I0715407

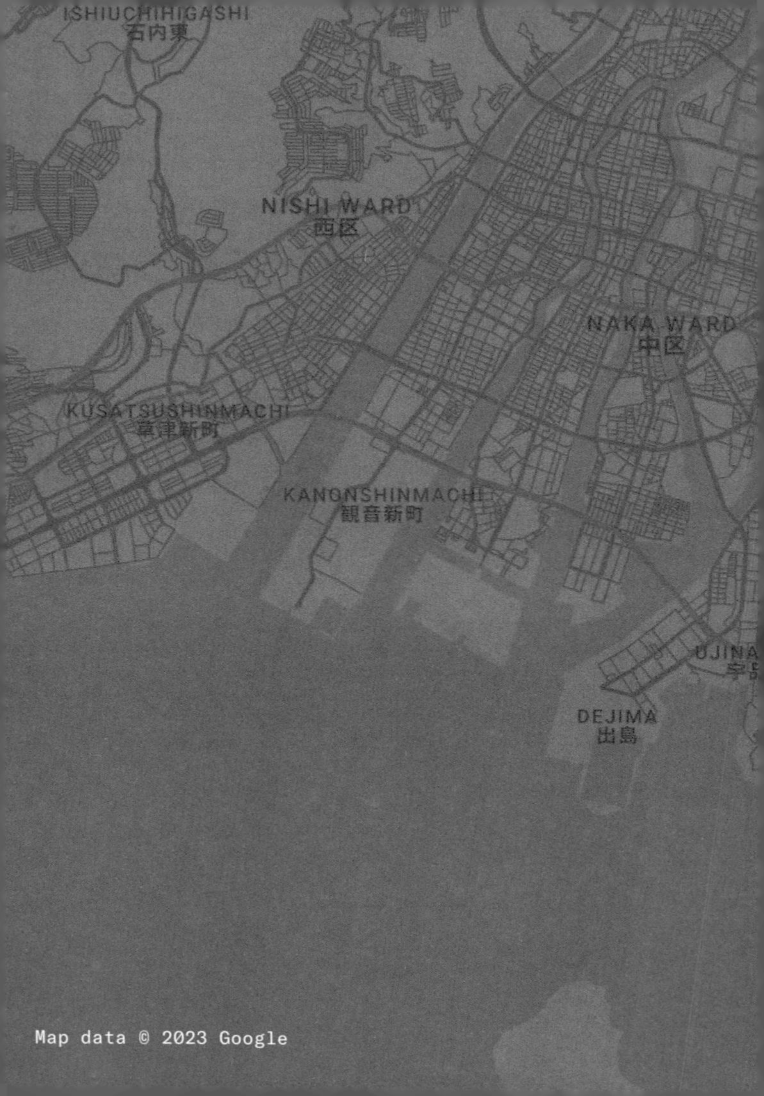

ISHIUCHIHIGASHI
石内東
NISHI WARD
西区
NAKA WARD
中区
KUSATSUSHINMACHI
草津新町
KANONSHINMACHI
観音新町
UJINA
宇品
DEJIMA
出島
Map data © 2023 Google

SOI BOOKS

MATSUBARACHO
松原町
Fuchu
府中町
FUNAKOSHIMINAMI
船越南
NAMI WARD
南区
N
KANONISHI
叶野西
HEISEIGAHAMA
平成ヶ浜
Saka
坂町

Soi Books / Stickerbomb Ltd

This publication has been realised exclusively
with the purpose and intent of a critical
and satirical documentation and discussion.
The views expressed in this publication are
those of the respective contributors and
are not necessarily shared by the publisher
and its staff.

Photography by SUIKO (@suiko1).
Design and layout by Ryo Sanada,
Suridh Hassan & SUIKO.

ISBN: 978-1-7397509-2-3
Printed in the U.K.

@bombstagram
www.stickerbombworld.com
www.soibooks.com

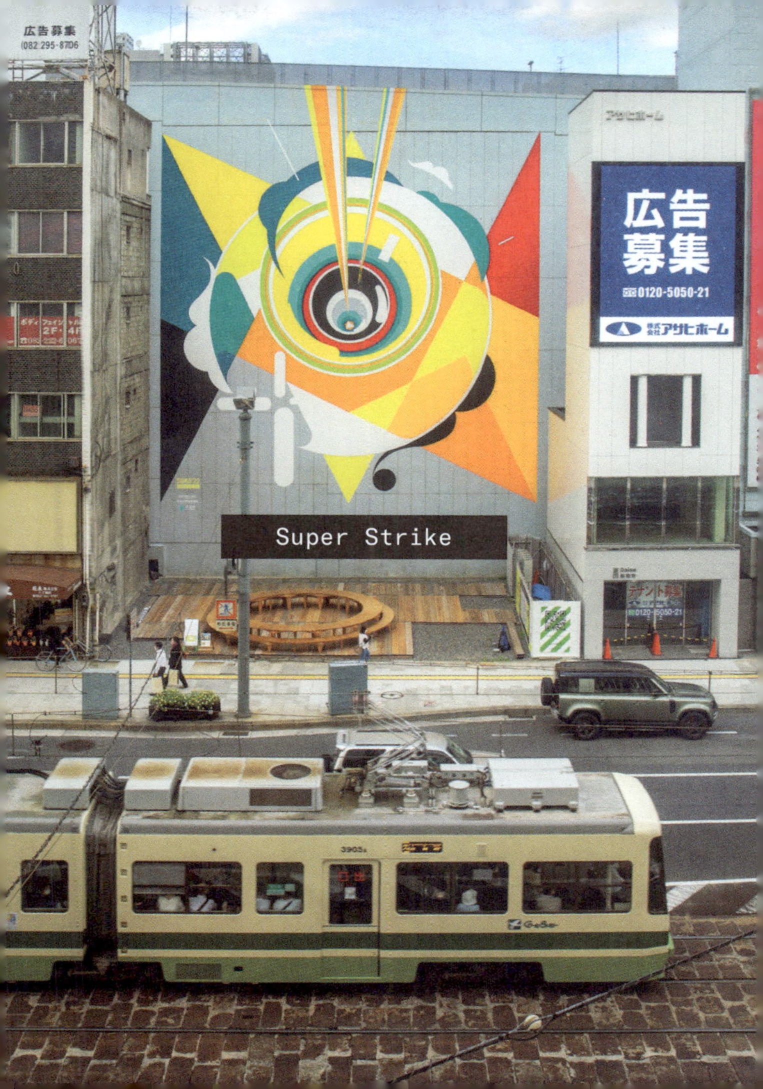

広告募集
(082 295-8706
広告
募集
0120-5050-21
株式会社アサヒホーム
Super Strike
テナント募集
0120-5050-21

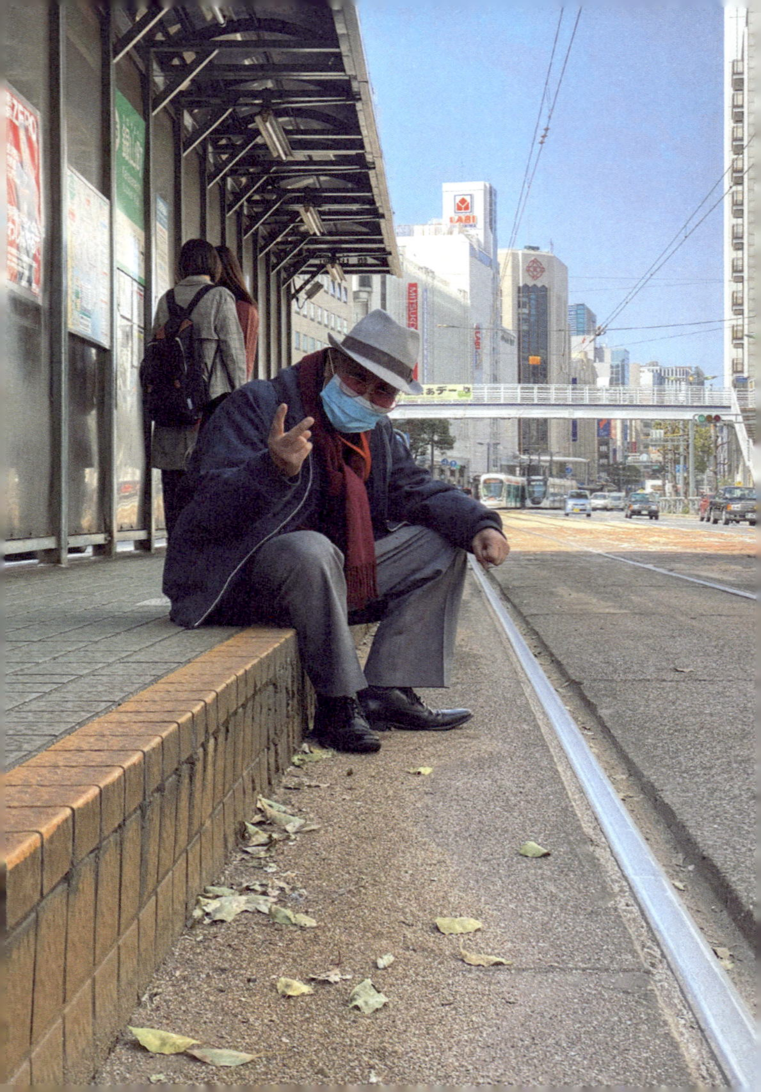

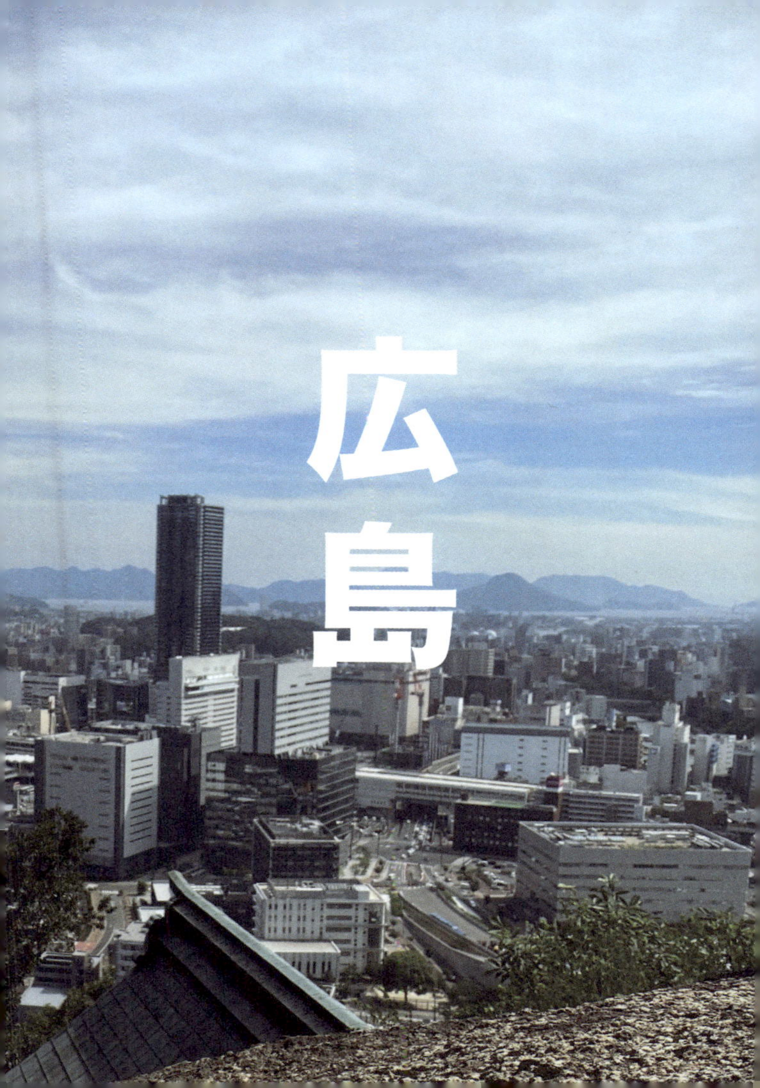

広島

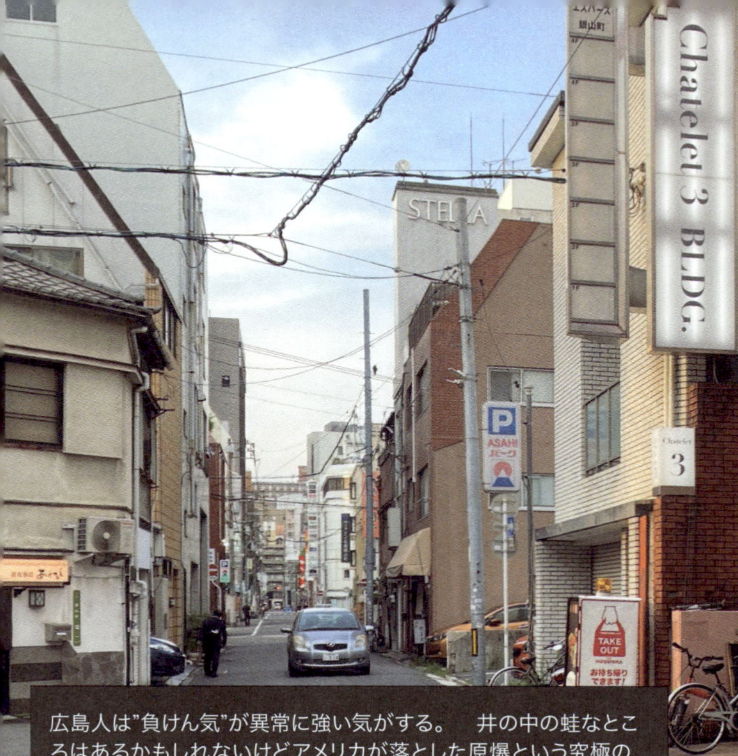

広島人は"負けん気"が異常に強い気がする。　井の中の蛙なところはあるかもしれないけどアメリカが落とした原爆という究極の暴力を喰らってもまだ立ち上がってきた底力。　ツッパリ力。
大都会に対しても負けん気で（勝手に）生きている。

I feel that people from Hiroshima have an unusually strong competitive spirit. We may be what others call 'frogs in a well', but we still have the strength to stand up even after suffering the ultimate violence of the atomic bomb dropped by the US.

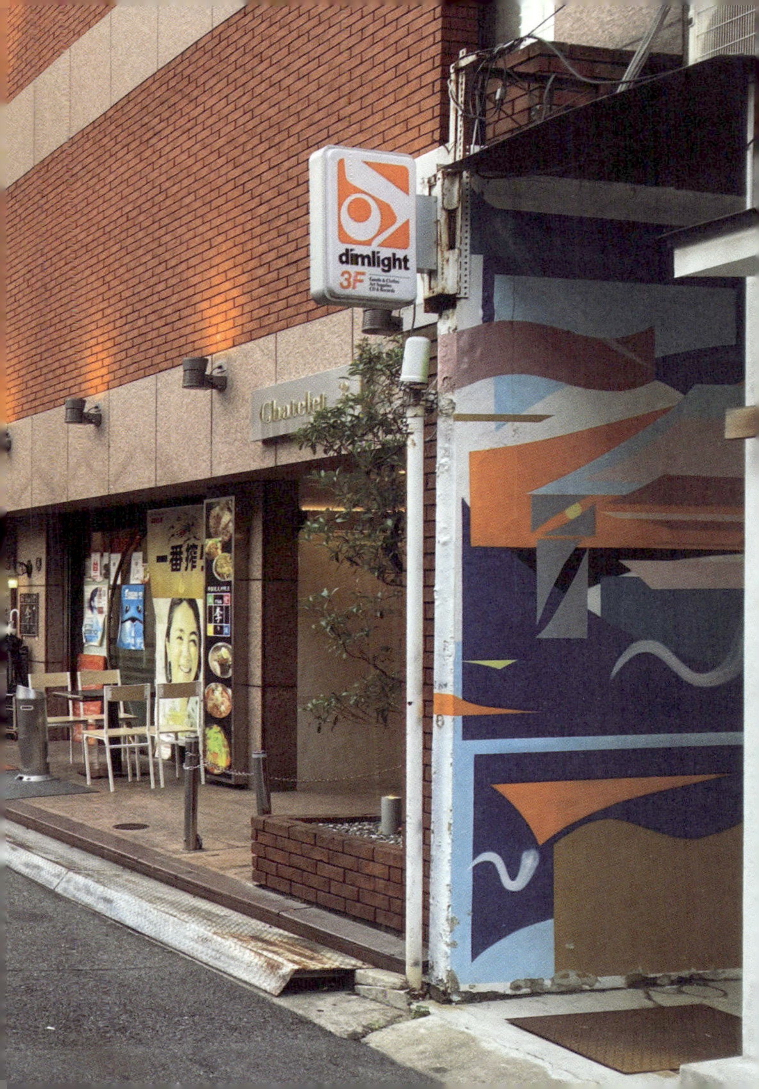

dimlight
3F
Goods & Coffee
Art Supplies
CD & Records
Chatelet

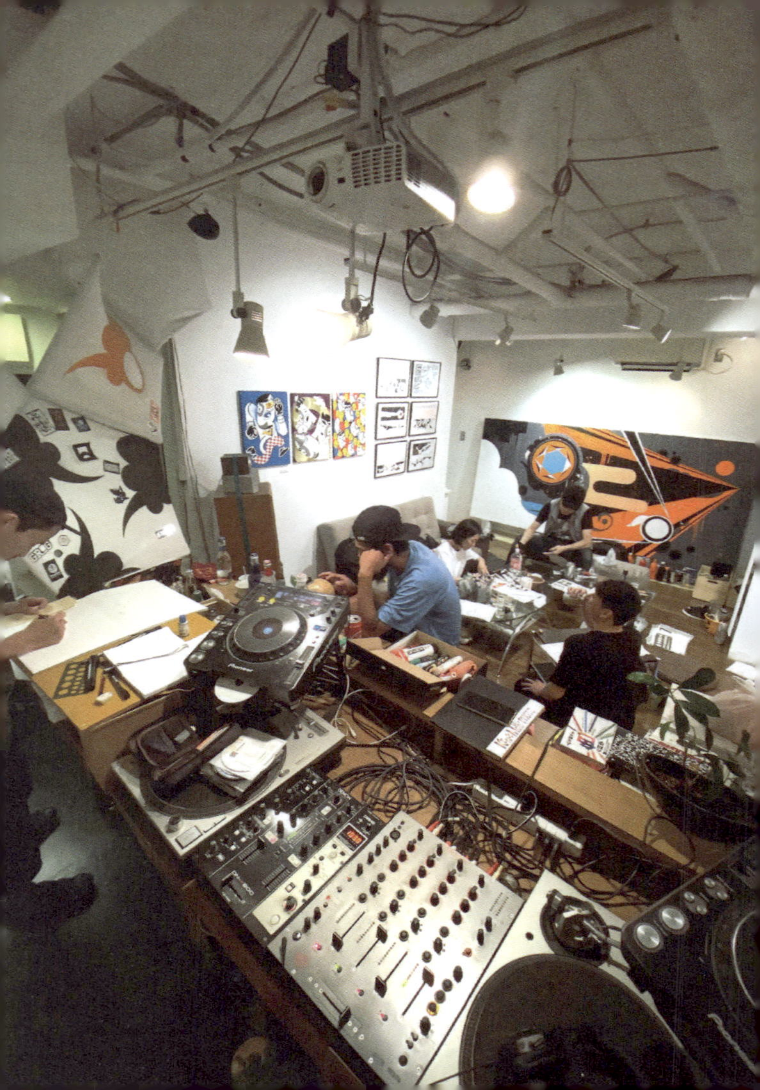

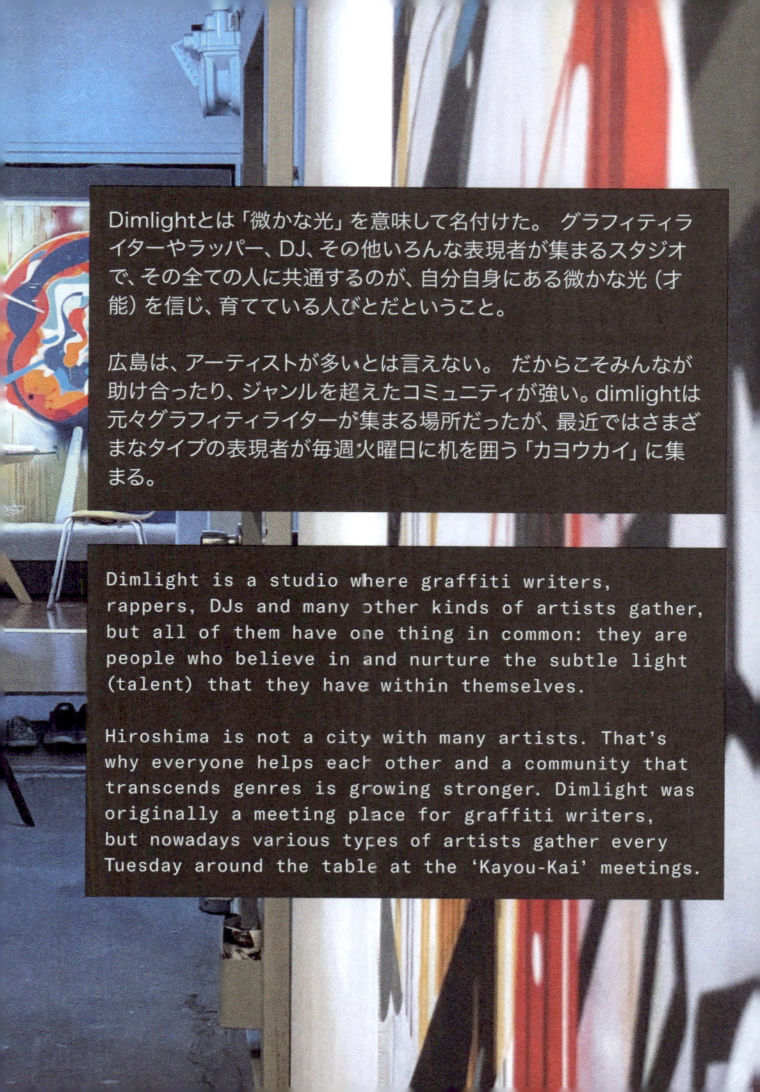

Dimlightとは「微かな光」を意味して名付けた。 グラフィティライターやラッパー、DJ、その他いろんな表現者が集まるスタジオで、その全ての人に共通するのが、自分自身にある微かな光（才能）を信じ、育てている人びとだということ。

広島は、アーティストが多いとは言えない。 だからこそみんなが助け合ったり、ジャンルを超えたコミュニティが強い。dimlightは元々グラフィティライターが集まる場所だったが、最近ではさまざまなタイプの表現者が毎週火曜日に机を囲う「カヨウカイ」に集まる。

Dimlight is a studio where graffiti writers, rappers, DJs and many other kinds of artists gather, but all of them have one thing in common: they are people who believe in and nurture the subtle light (talent) that they have within themselves.

Hiroshima is not a city with many artists. That's why everyone helps each other and a community that transcends genres is growing stronger. Dimlight was originally a meeting place for graffiti writers, but nowadays various types of artists gather every Tuesday around the table at the 'Kayou-Kai' meetings.

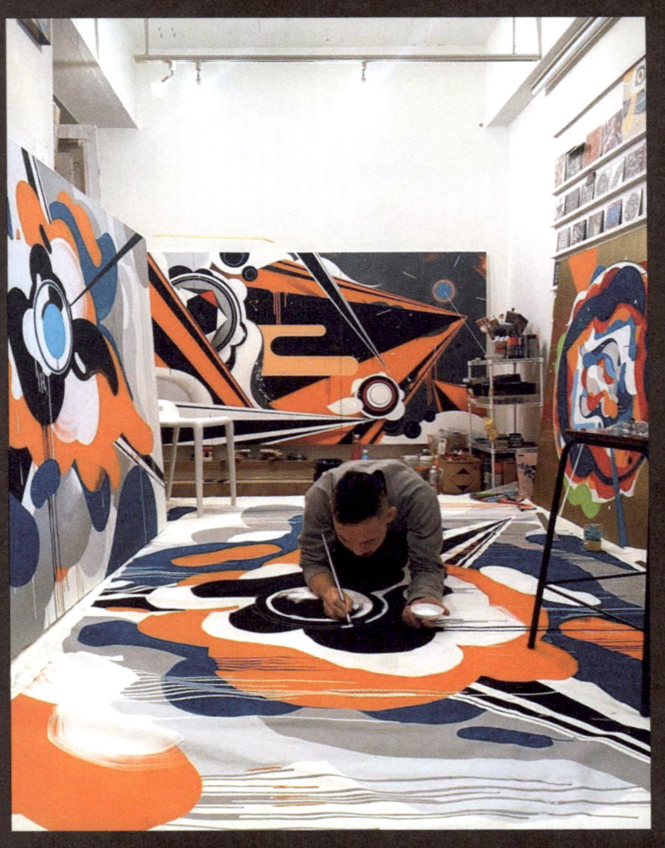

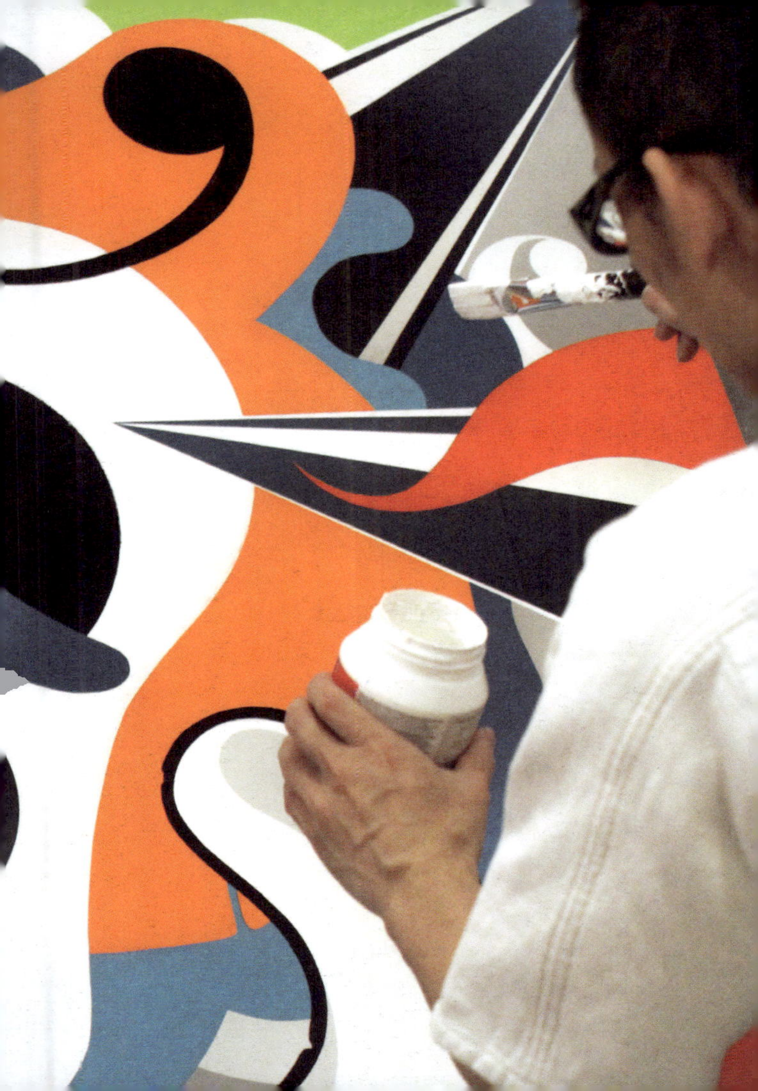

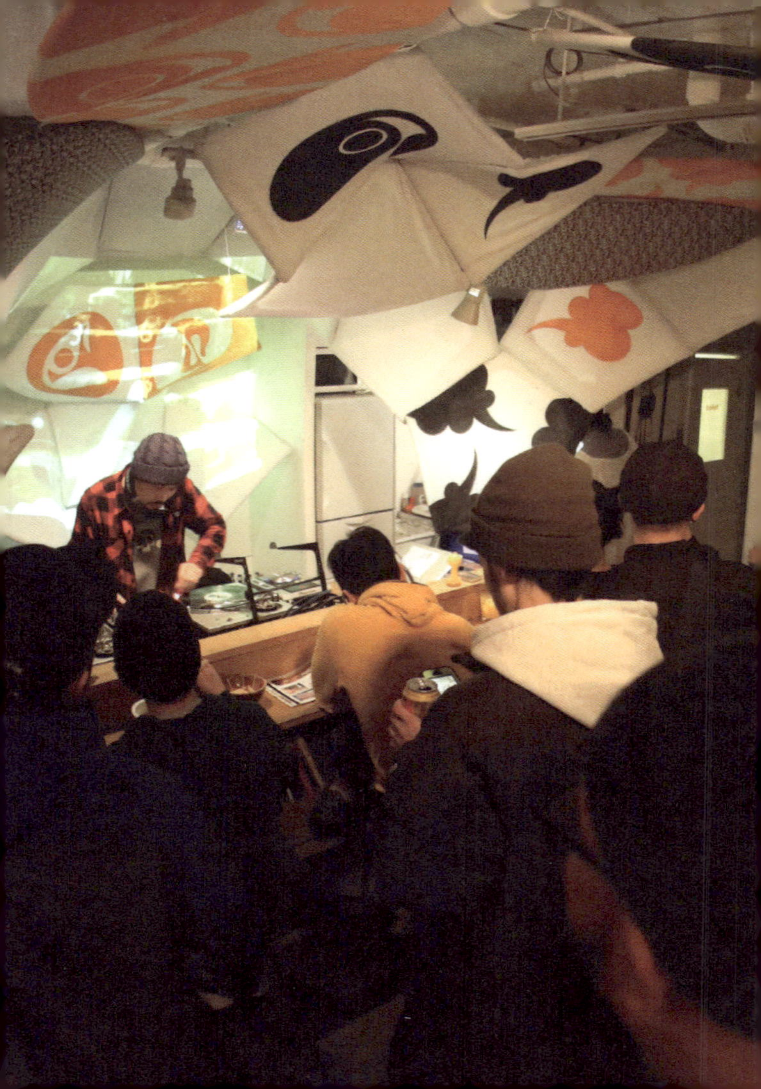

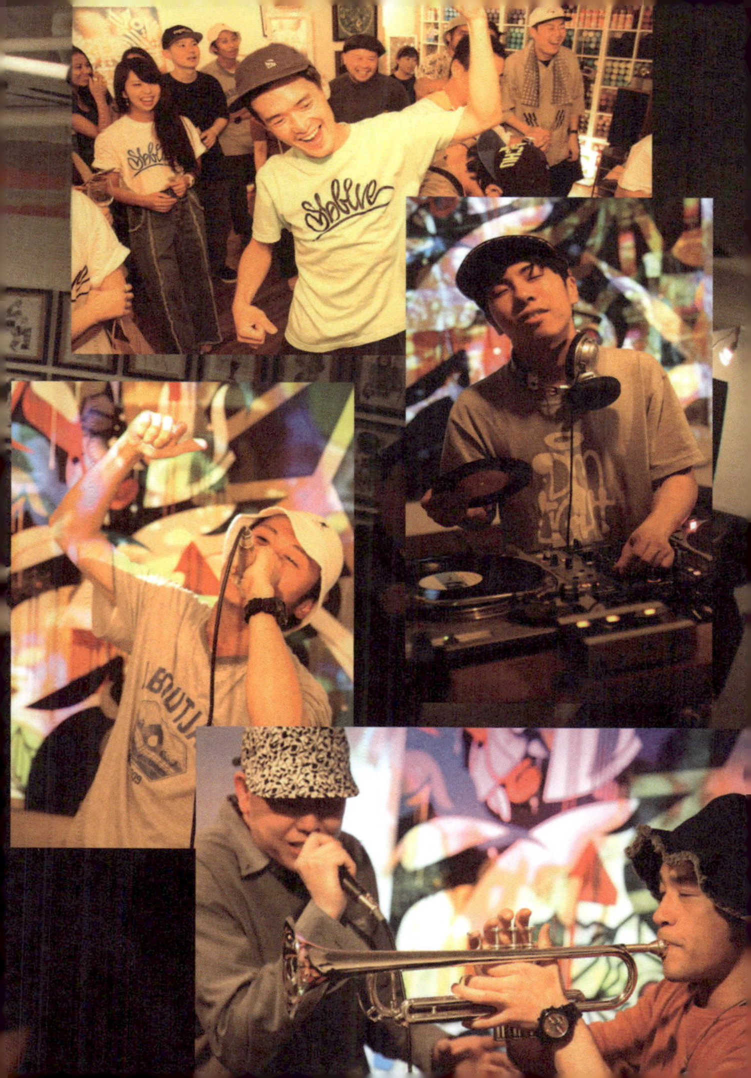

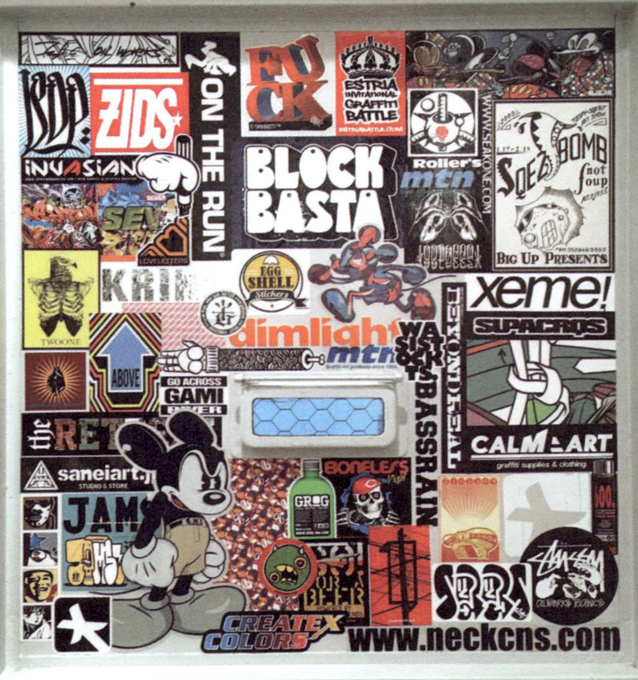

ZIDS
INVASIAN
LOVELETTERS
ON THE RUN
BU CK
ESTRIA
INVITATIONAL
GRAFFITI
BATTLE
BLOCK
BASTA
Roller's
mtn
SQEZ BOMB
not
foup
Big Up Presents
KRIN
EGG
SHELL
Stickers
TWOONE
ABOVE
dimlight
mtn
GO ACROSS
GAMI
xeme!
SUPACROS
BEYOND REAL
CALM ART
graffiti supplies & clothing.
the RET
saneiart.
STUDIO & STORE
JAMS
BONELESS
GROG
OUR BEER
WATAMBASSRAIN
CREATEX
COLORS
www.neckcns.com

OILWORKS
saneiart.
STUDIO & STORE
ABOVE
INVASIAN
HKWALLS
POWERED BY
THE GRAFF INK
BROCK BUSTA
CALM
WRITERS
WRITERS
ZAKAT
calma
www.deeeznut
Roid

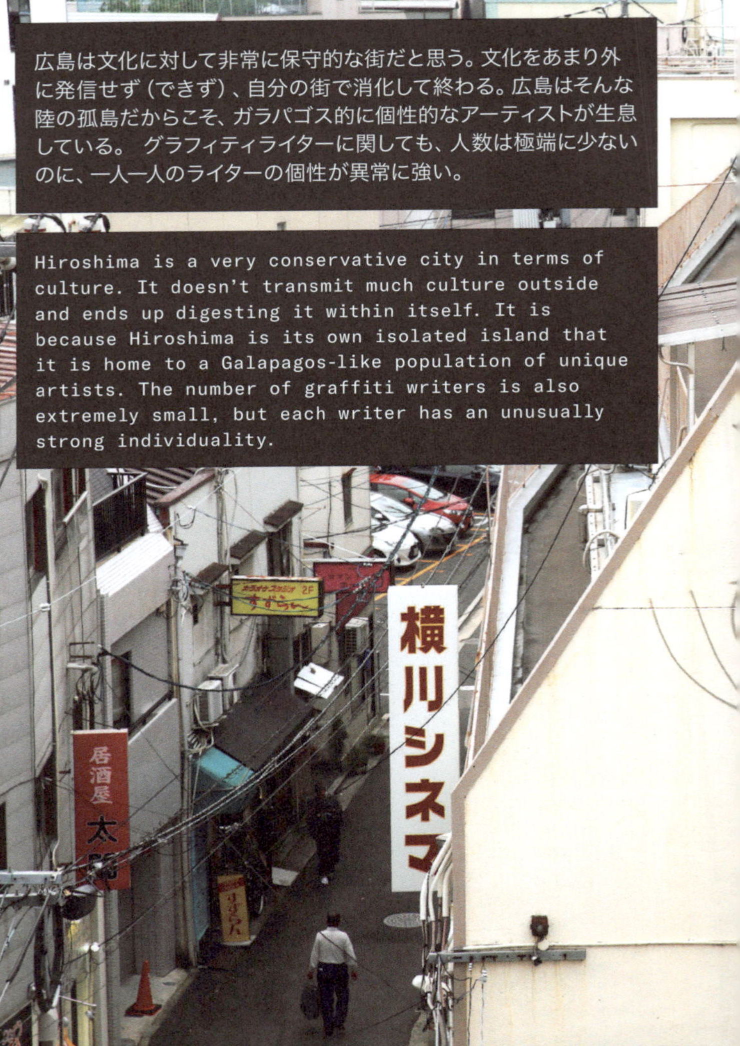

広島は文化に対して非常に保守的な街だと思う。文化をあまり外に発信せず（できず）、自分の街で消化して終わる。広島はそんな陸の孤島だからこそ、ガラパゴス的に個性的なアーティストが生息している。 グラフィティライターに関しても、人数は極端に少ないのに、一人一人のライターの個性が異常に強い。

Hiroshima is a very conservative city in terms of culture. It doesn't transmit much culture outside and ends up digesting it within itself. It is because Hiroshima is its own isolated island that it is home to a Galapagos-like population of unique artists. The number of graffiti writers is also extremely small, but each writer has an unusually strong individuality.

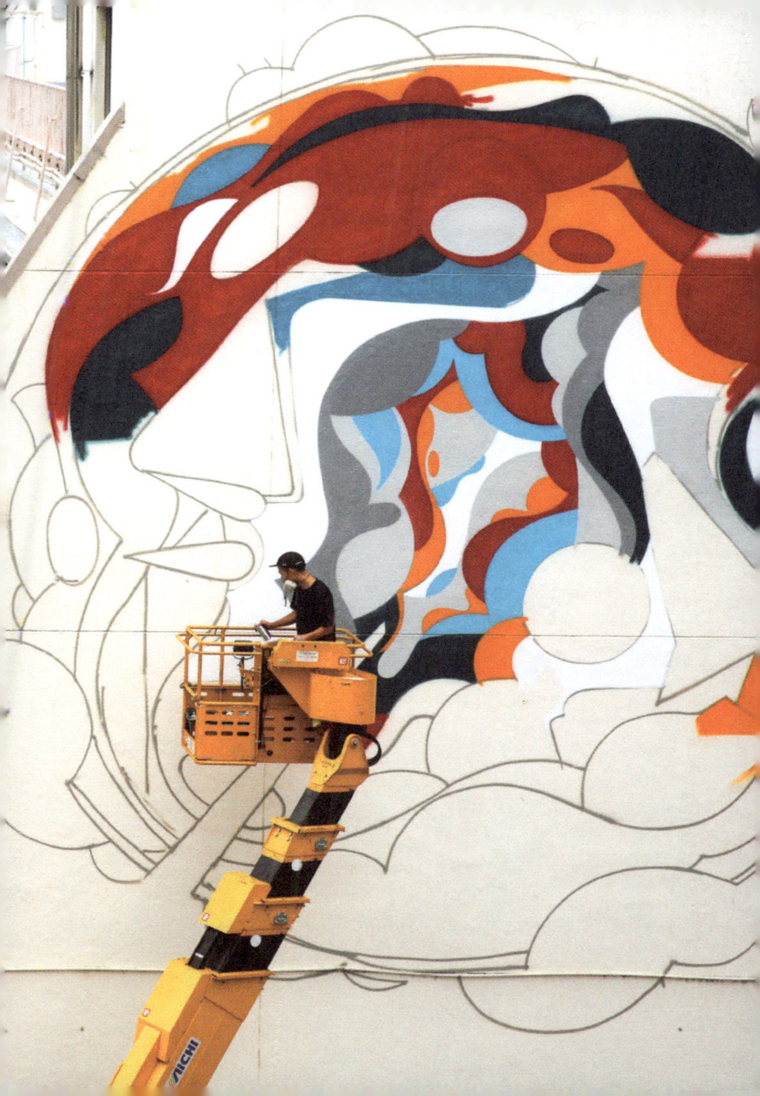

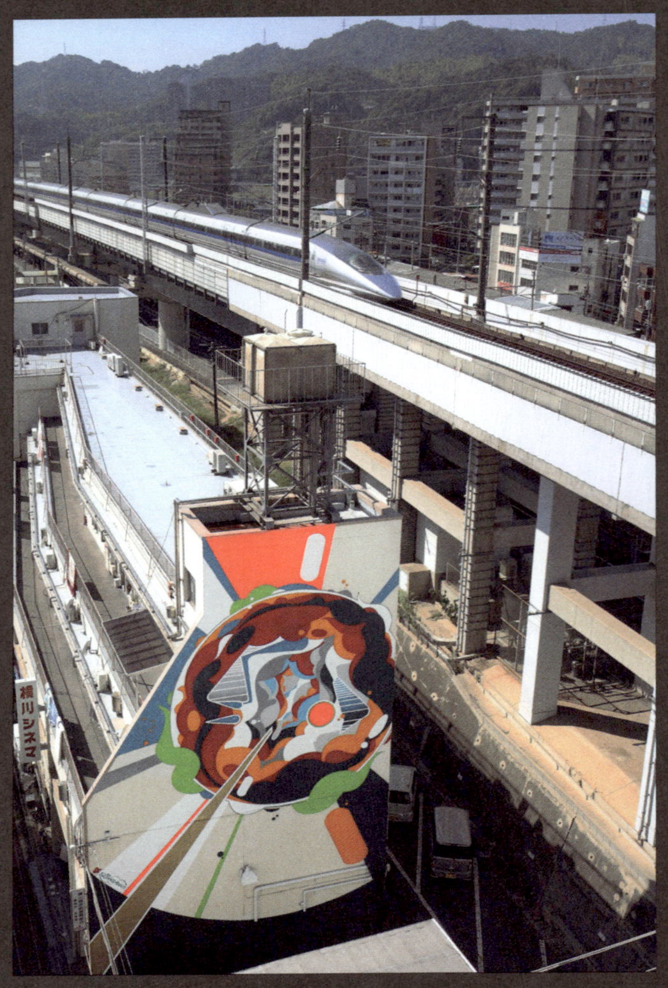

"NANOHANA" / Hiroshima, 2017

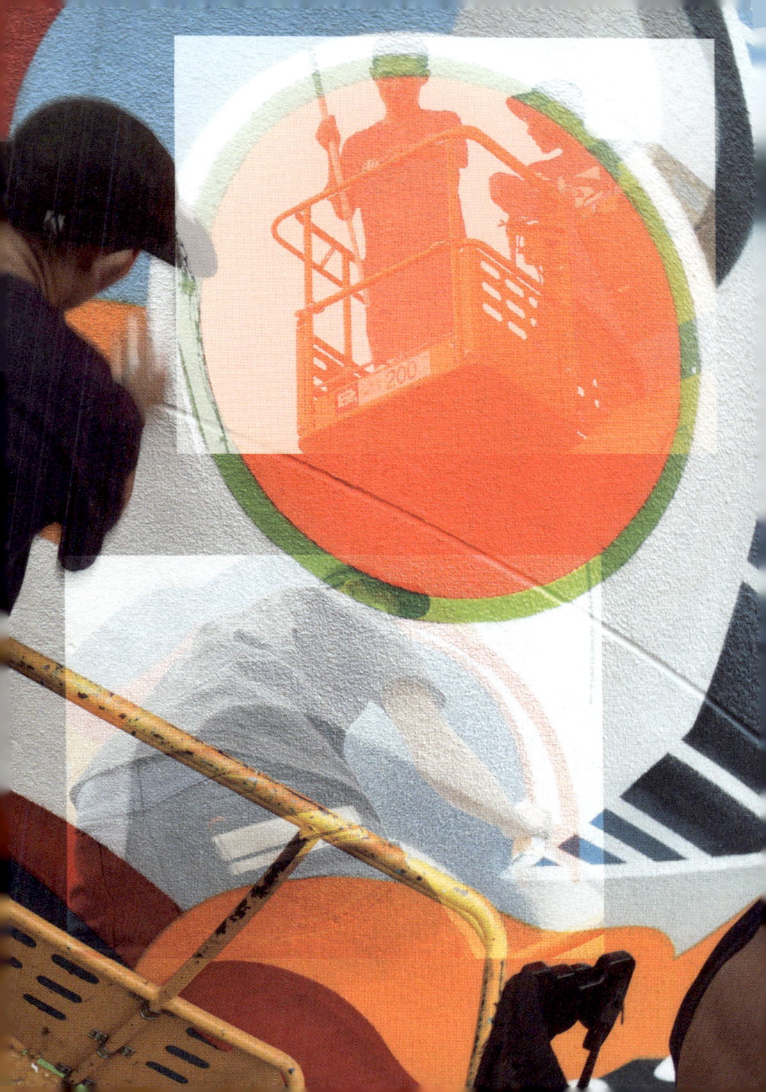

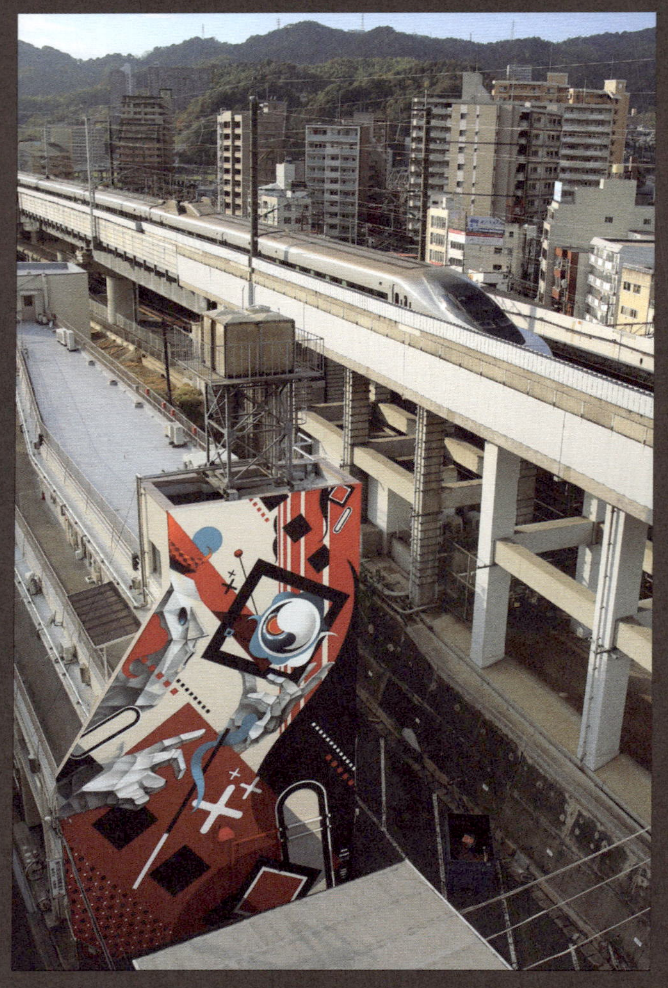

"TAMA" / SUIKO, FATE & imaone, Hiroshima, 2020

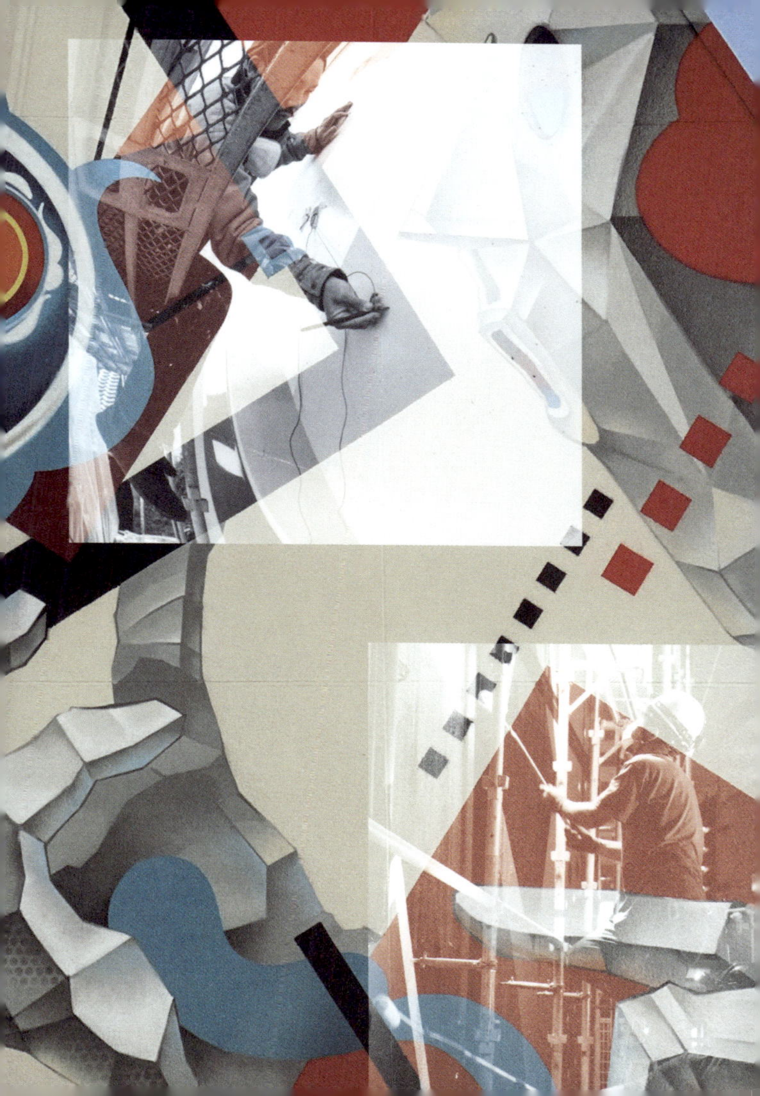

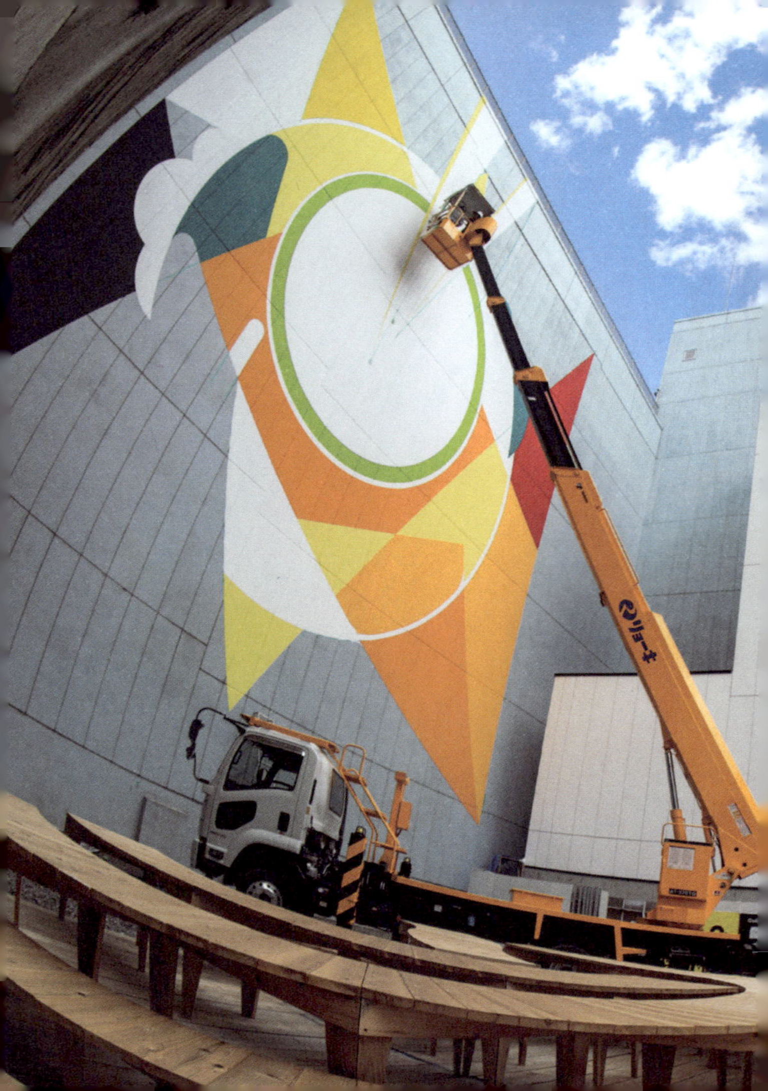

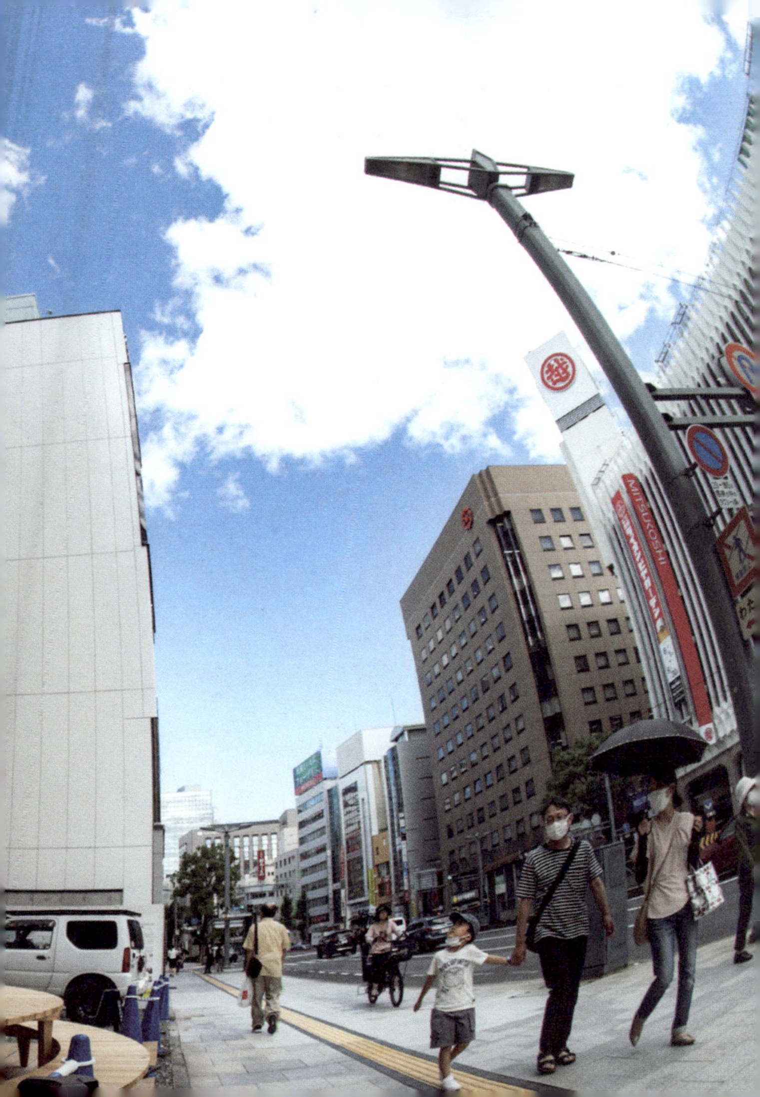

MITSUKOSHI

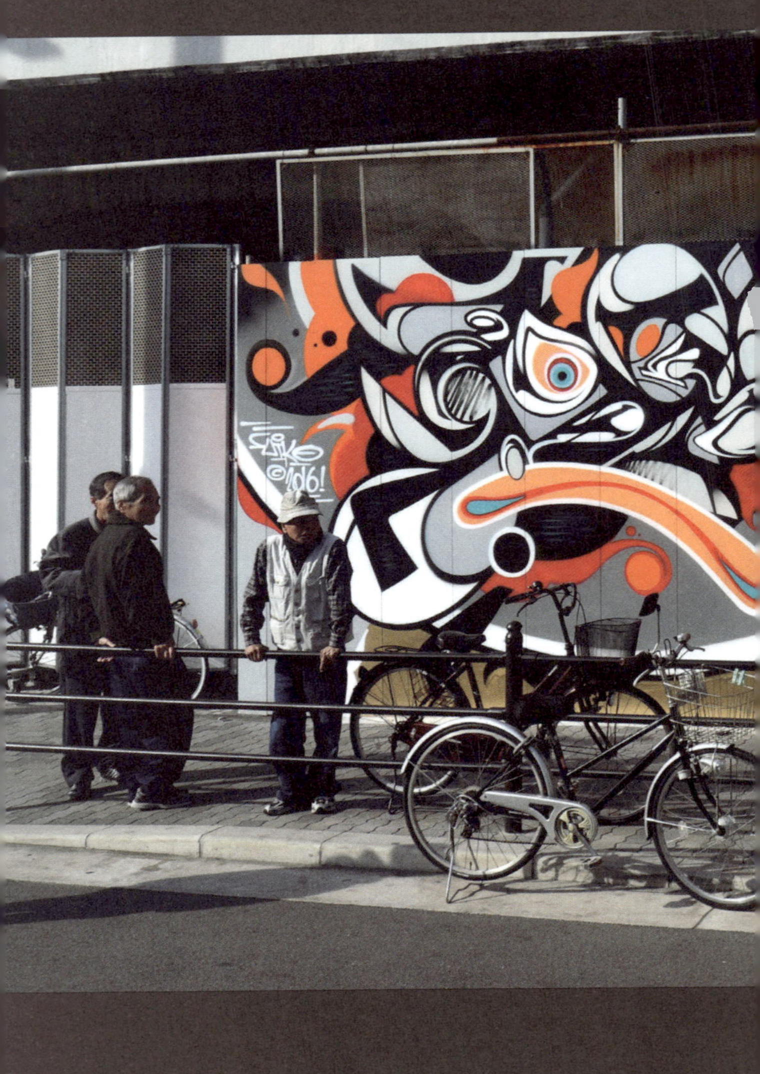

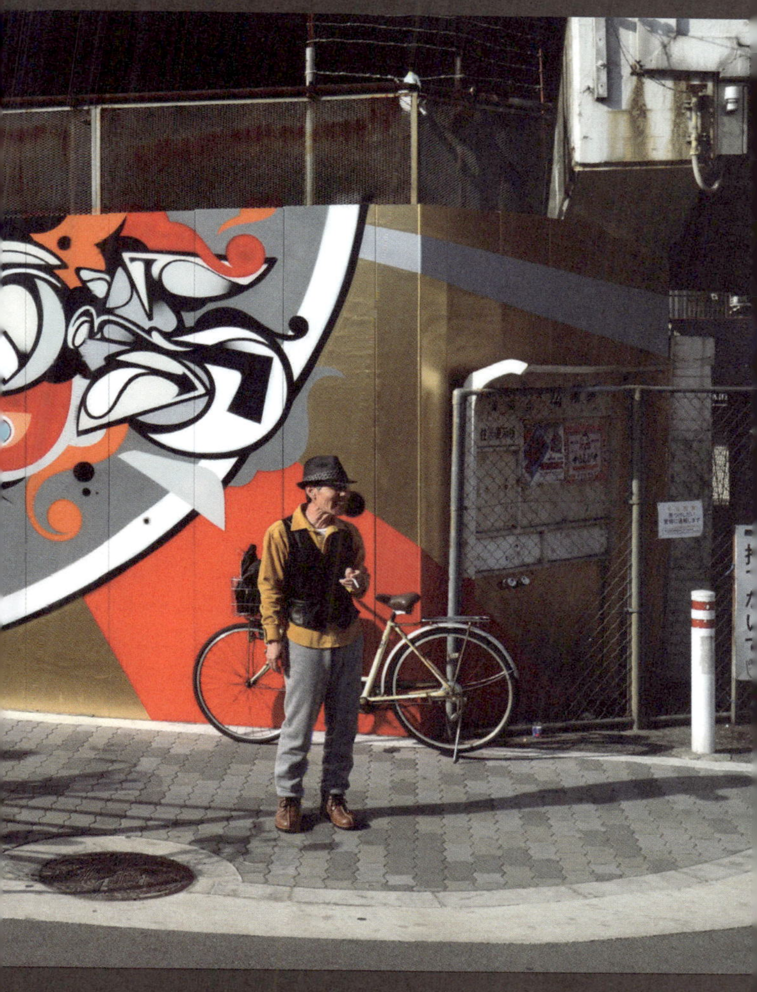

"KABUKIDAMA" / Osaka, 2016

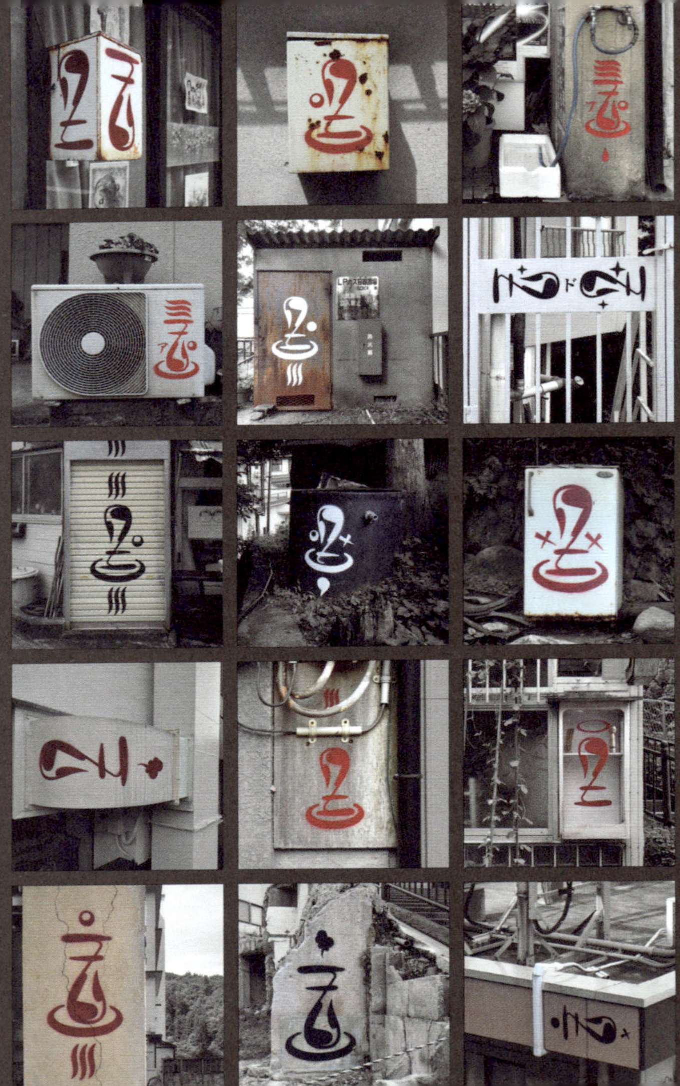

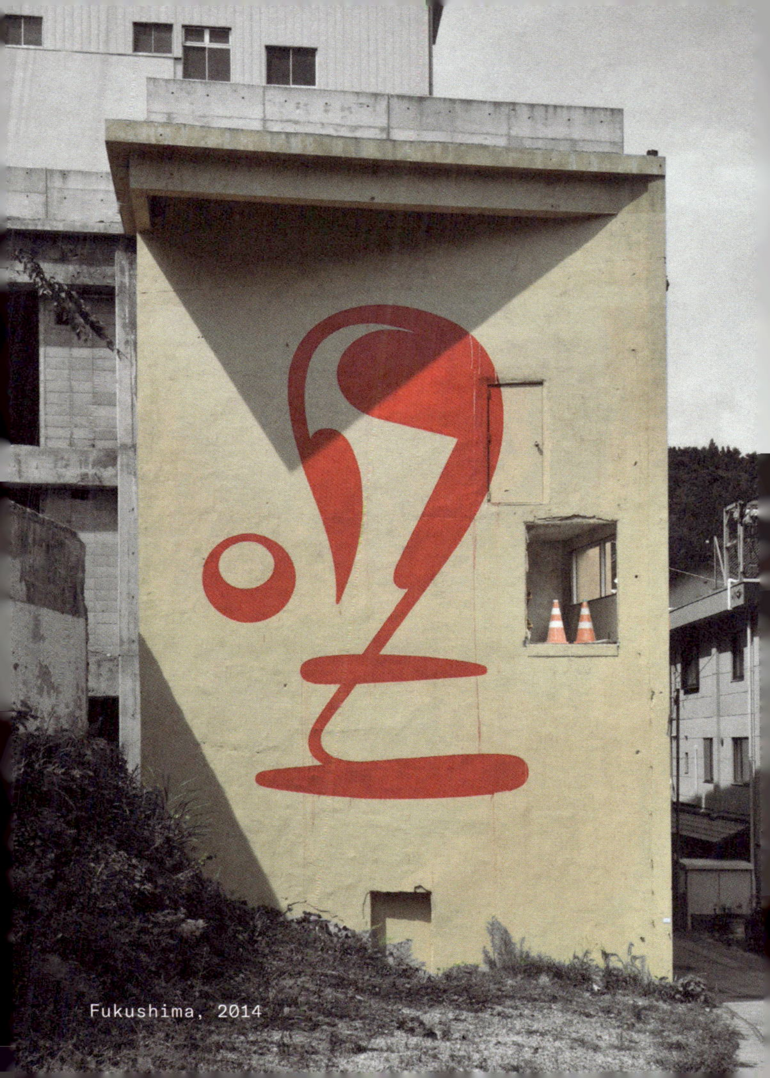

Fukushima, 2014

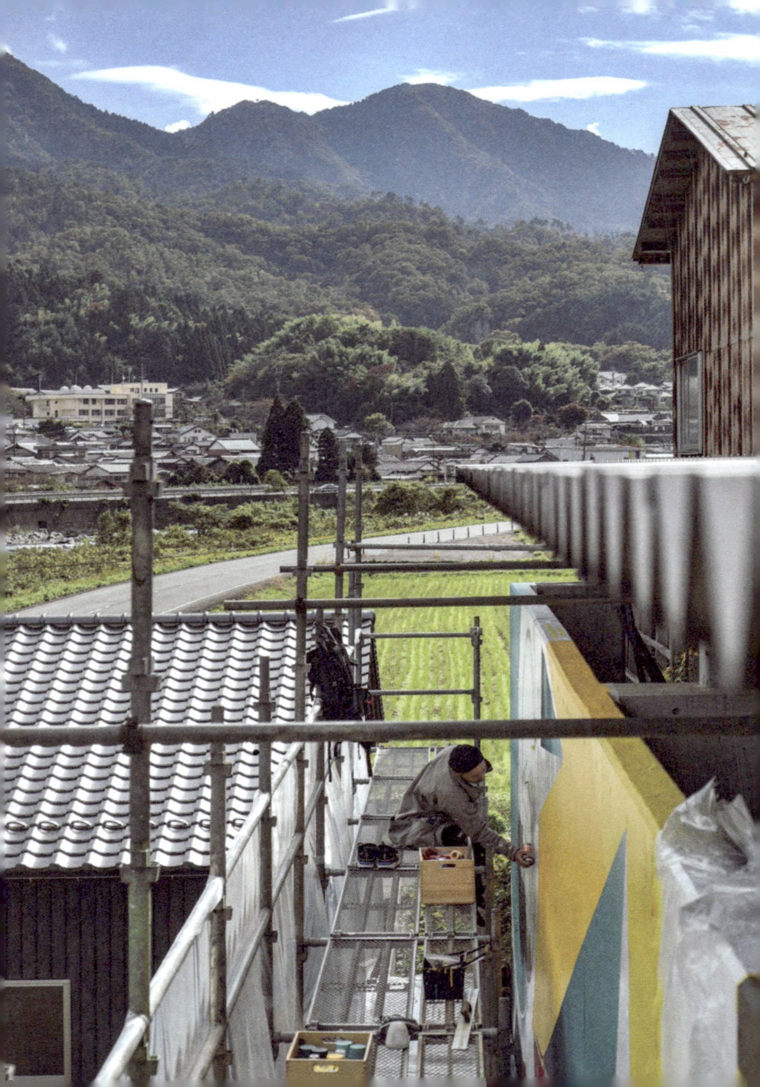

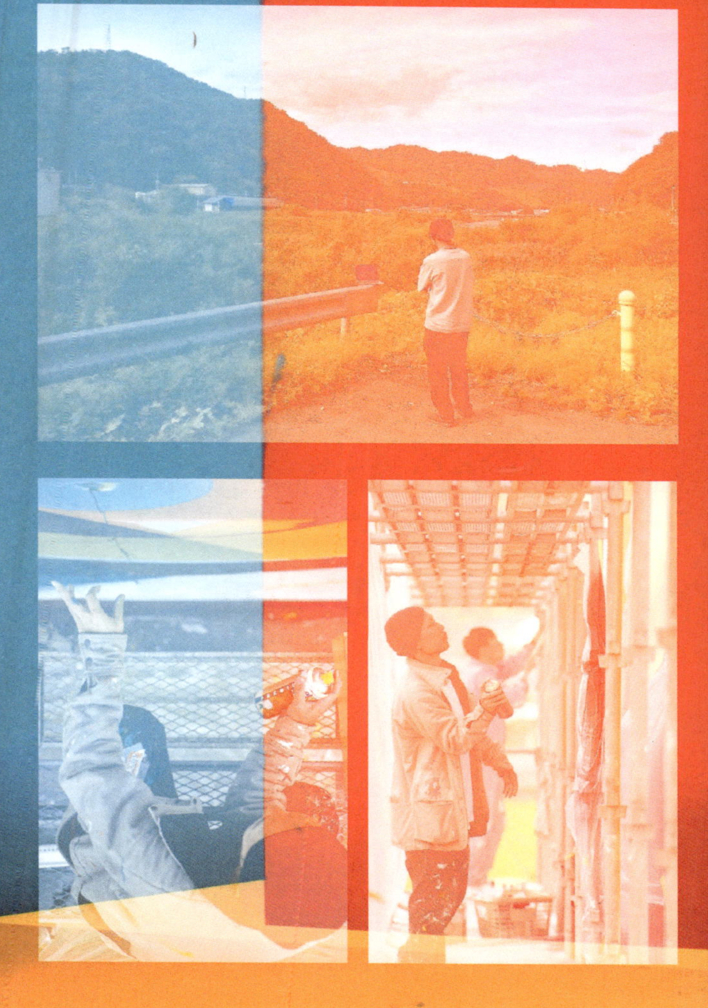

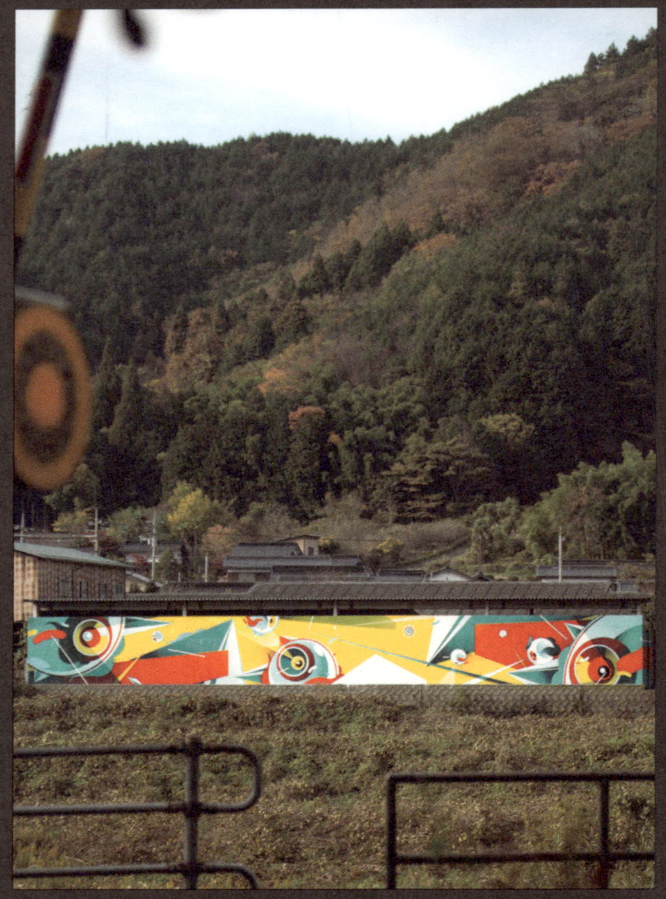

Tottori, 2021

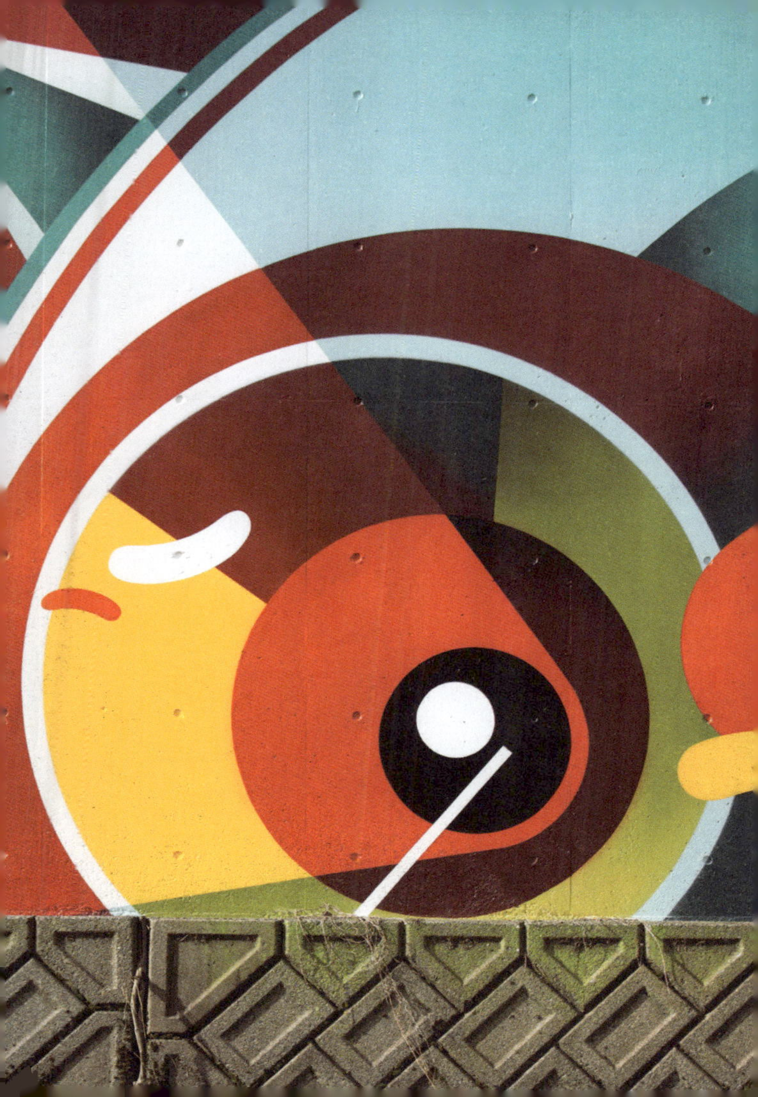

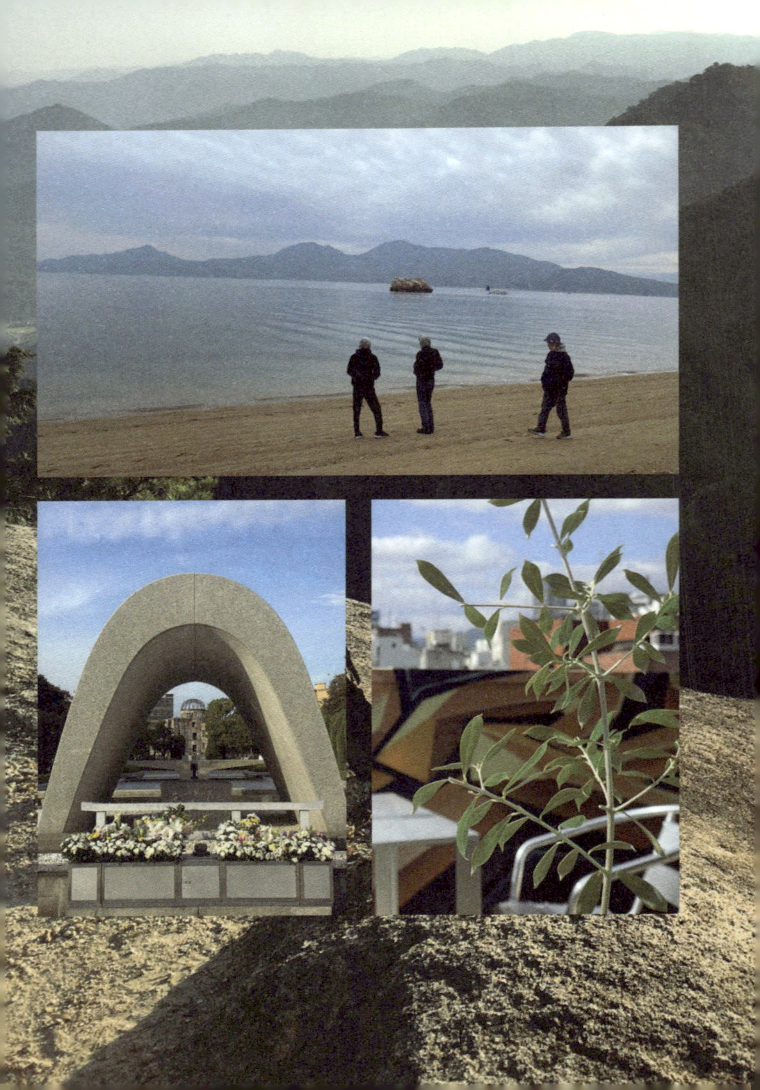

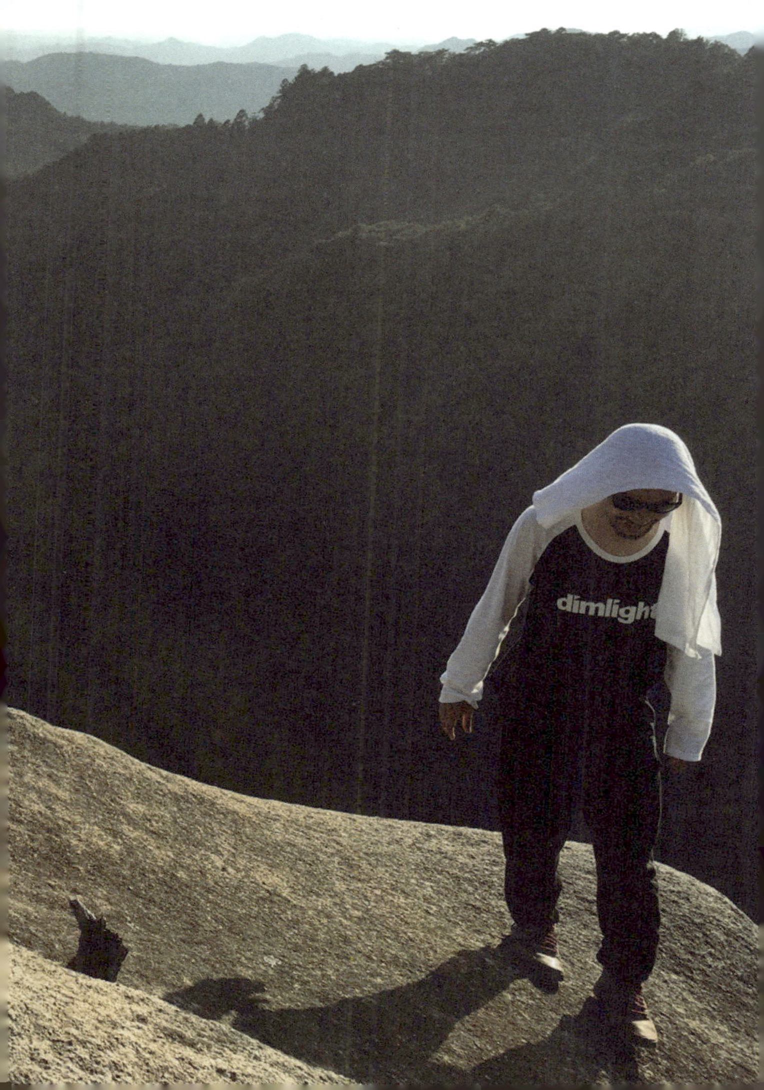

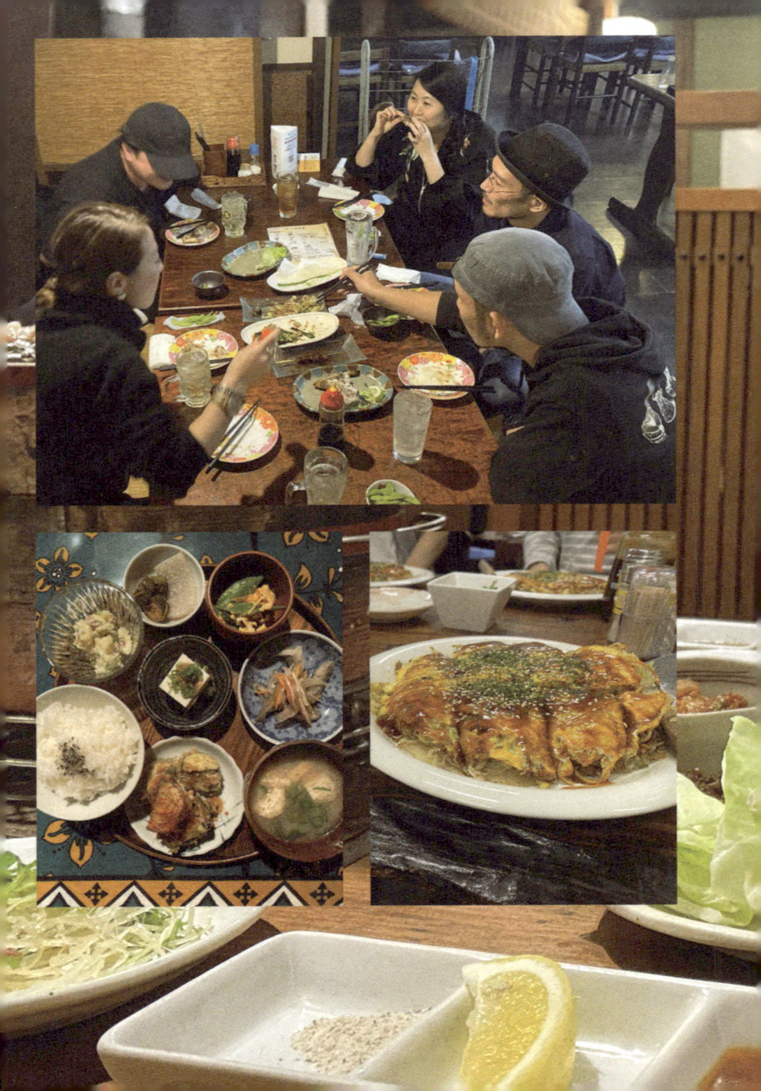

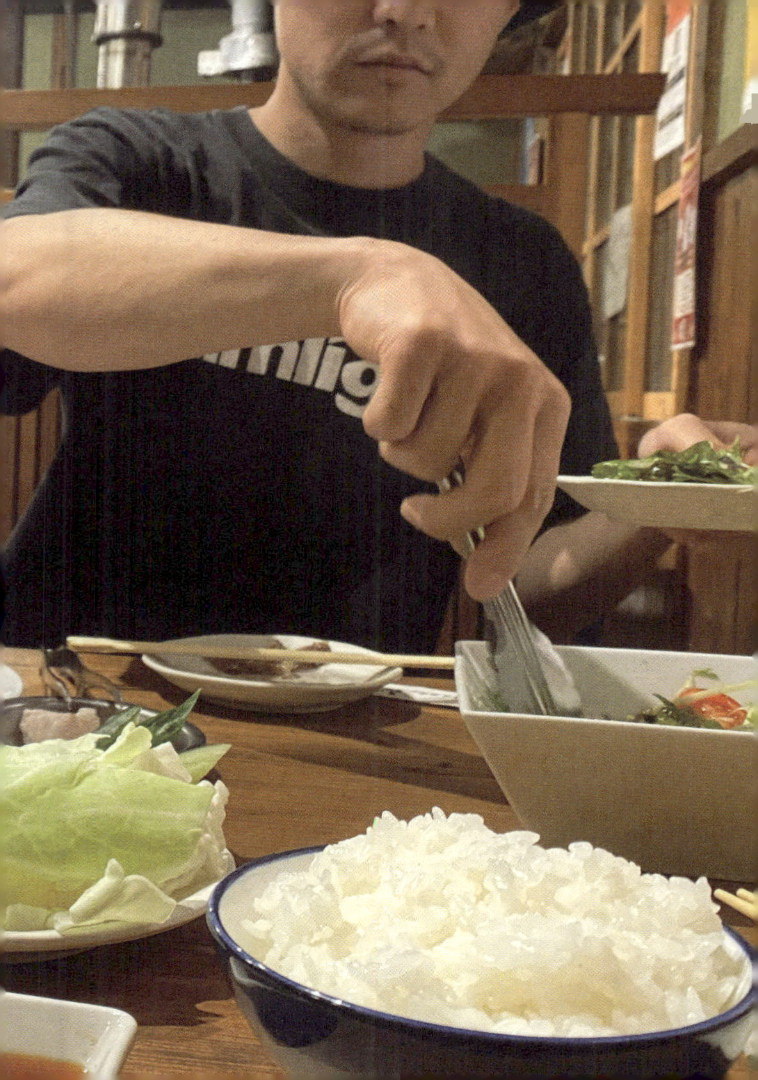

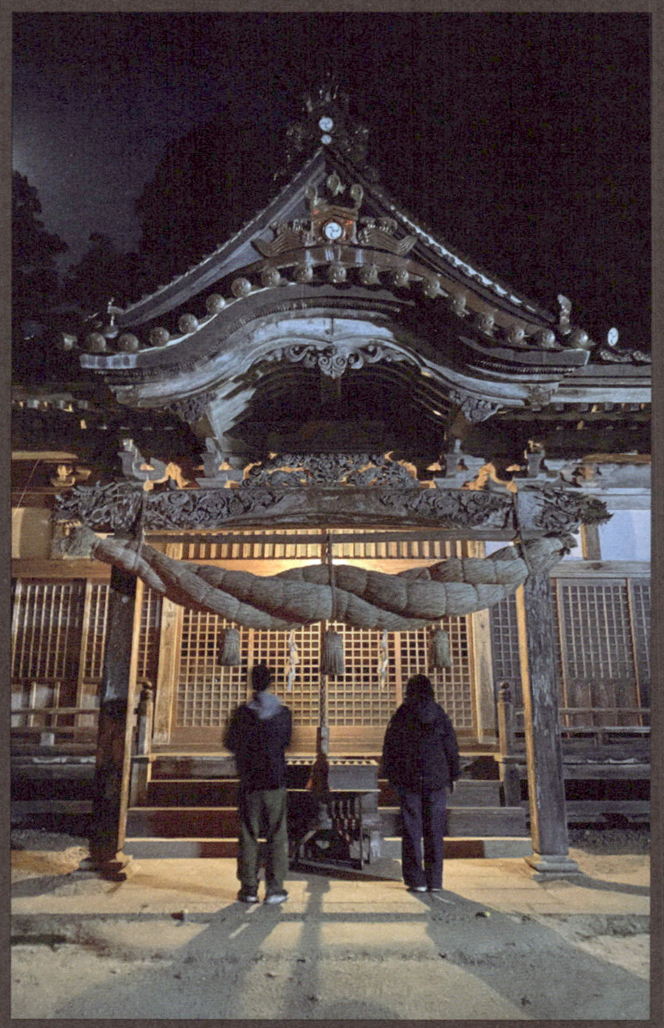

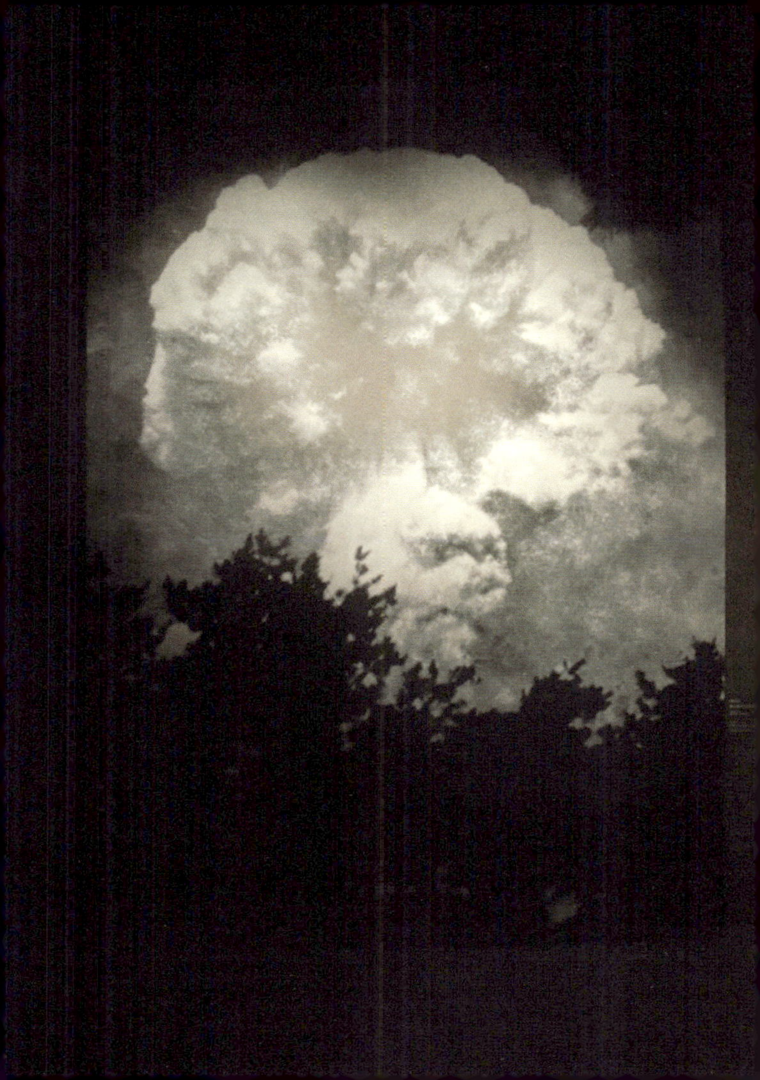

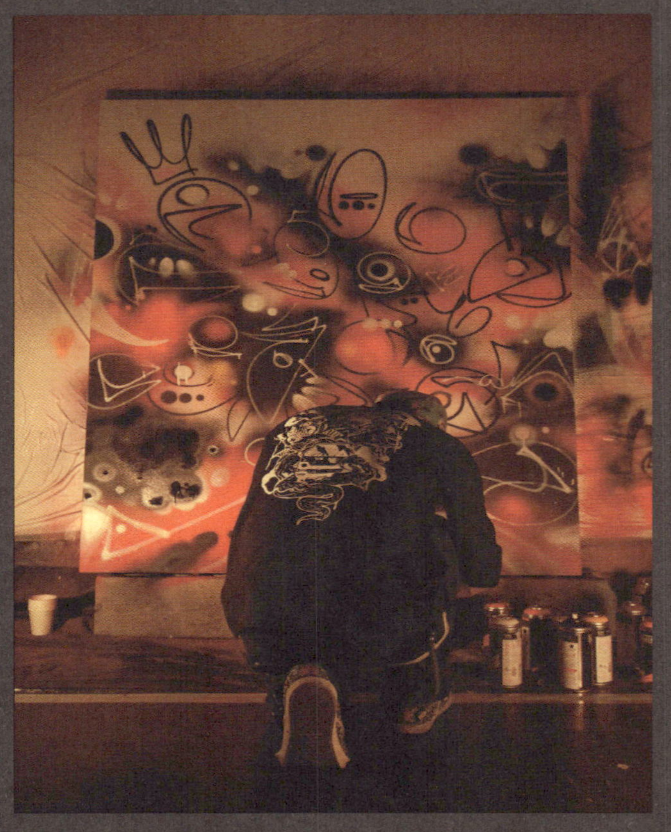

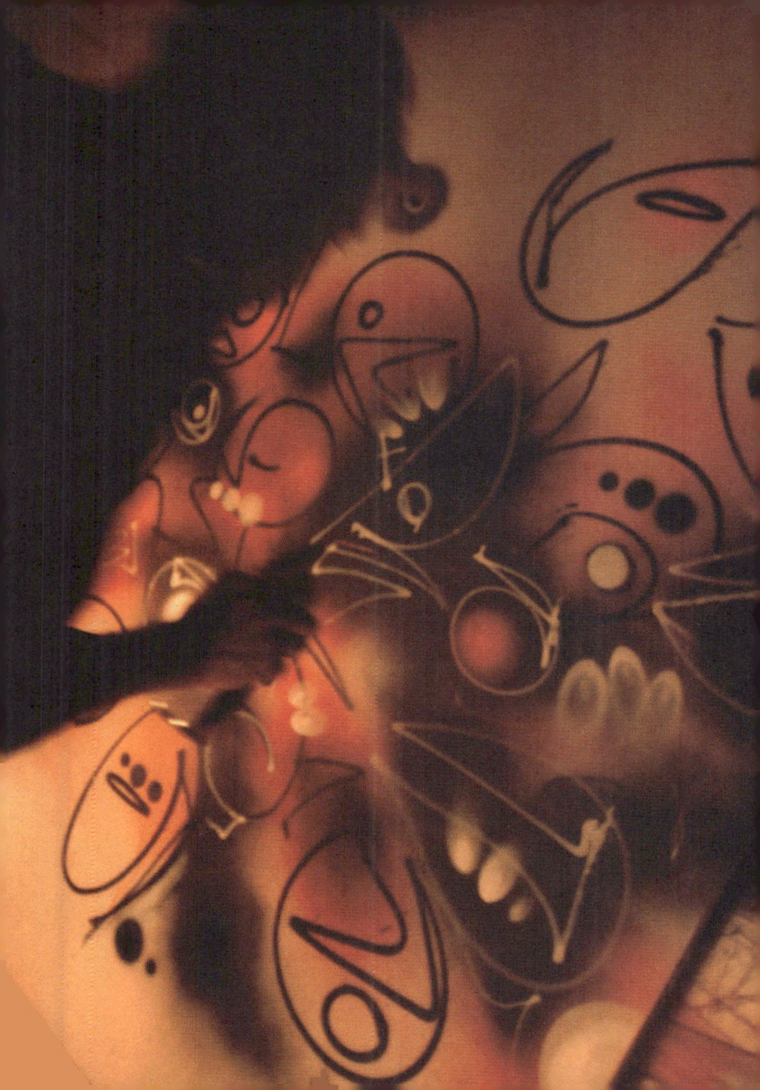

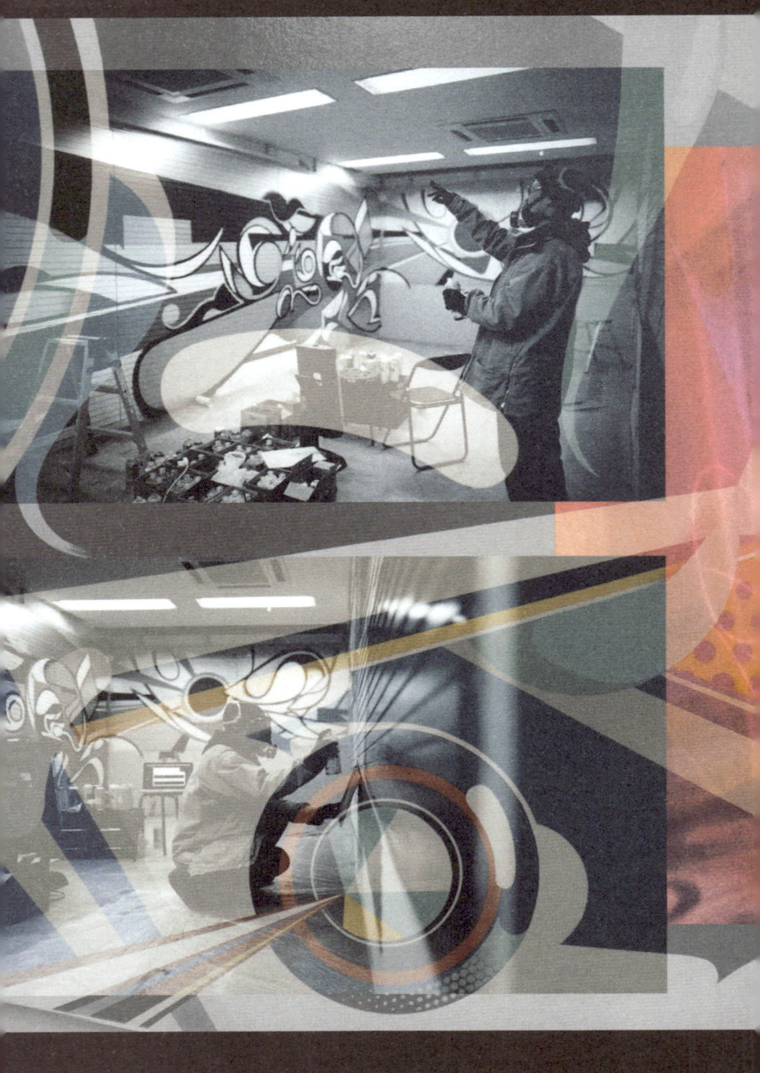

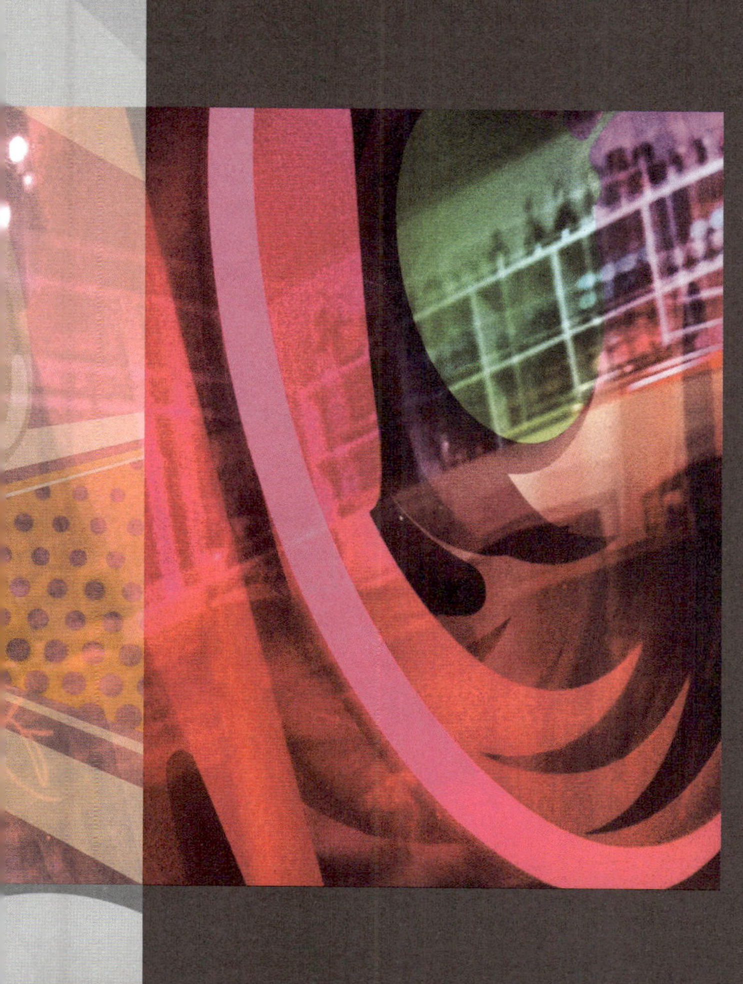

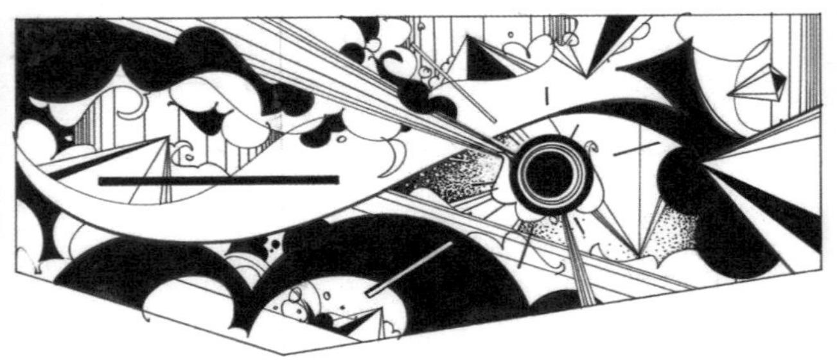

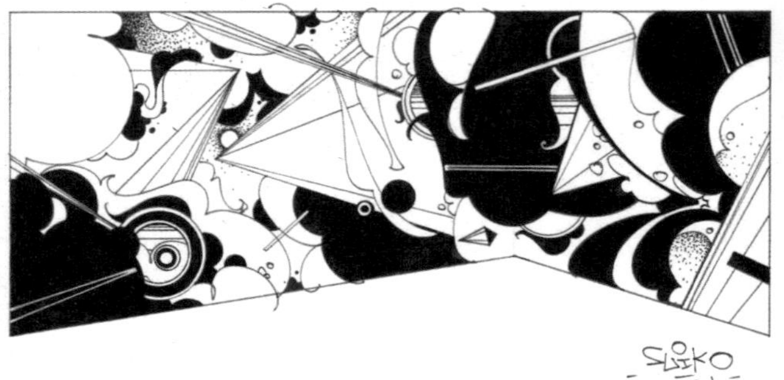

"INTROSPECTION" & "EXECUTION" / Hiroshima, 2021

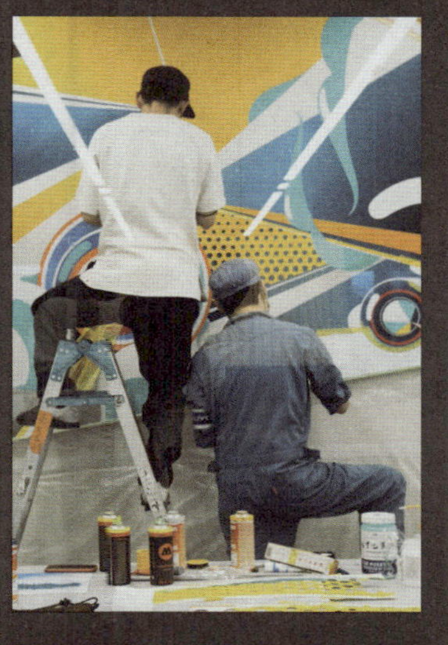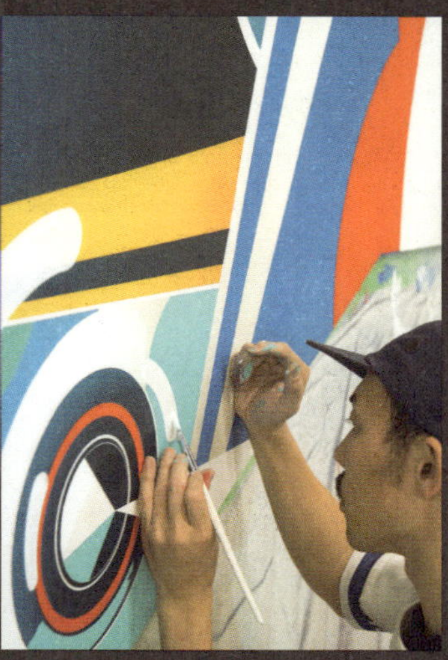

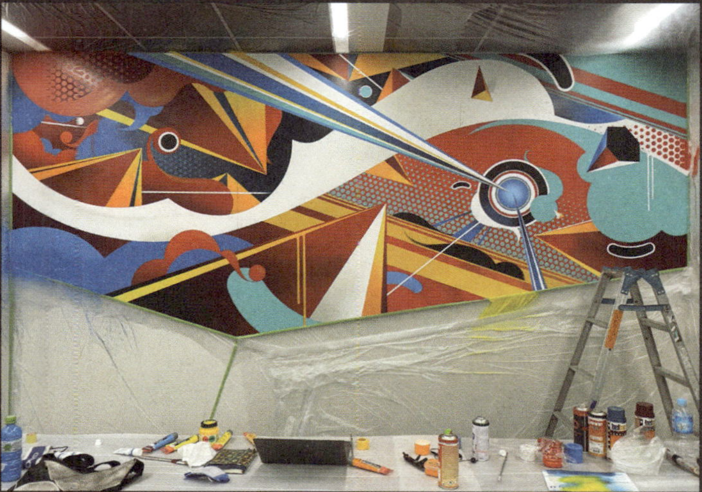

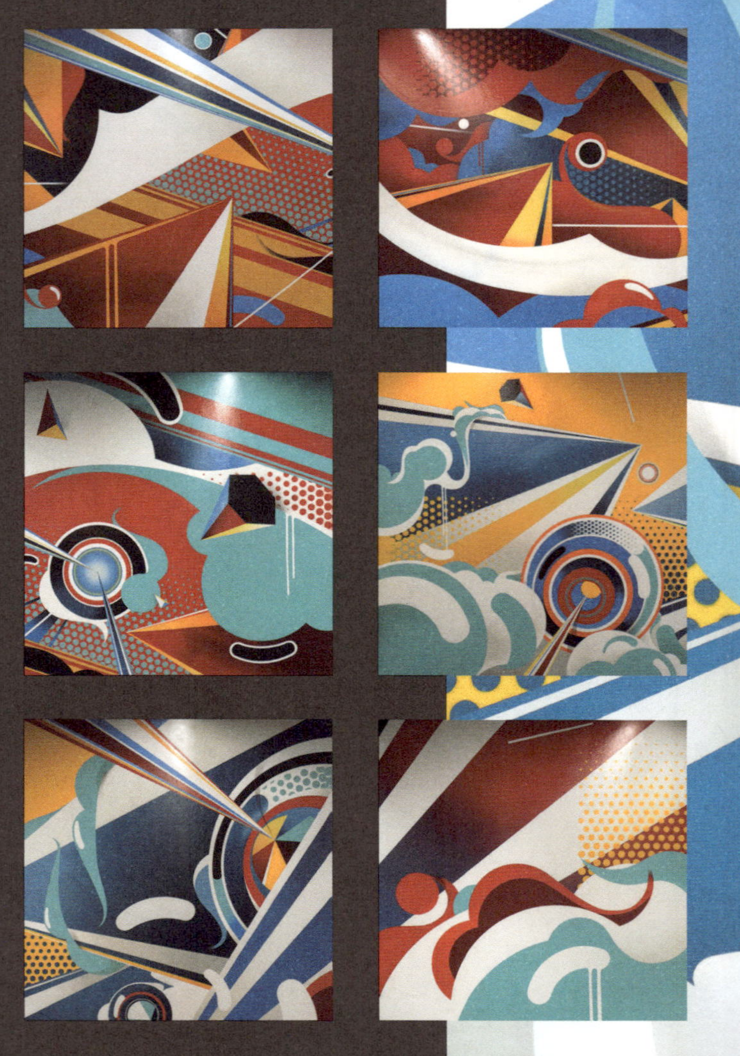

広島の人々は汚れたものや暴力的なものを嫌う傾向があると思う。 それは原爆という、極限的にネガティブを土台にした街だから。 そんな街で表現活動をする上で、自分のアートのスタイルはクリーンでポジティブな色面になっていくことが自然と生き残る方法だった気がする。

I think the people of Hiroshima tend to dislike anything they consider dirty or violent. This is because it is a city that rebuilt itself upon the horrific nihilism of the atomic bomb. I feel that the natural way for my art to survive in such a city is for the style to become refined and more positive.

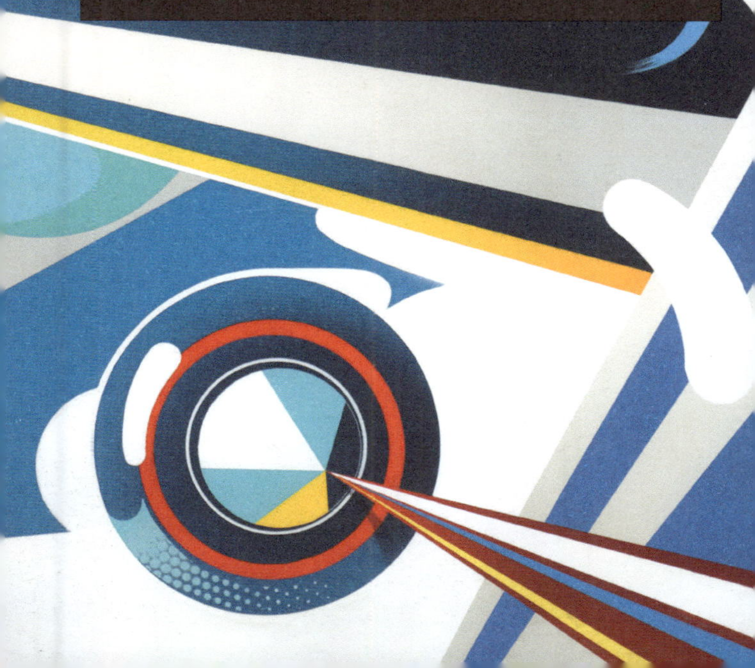

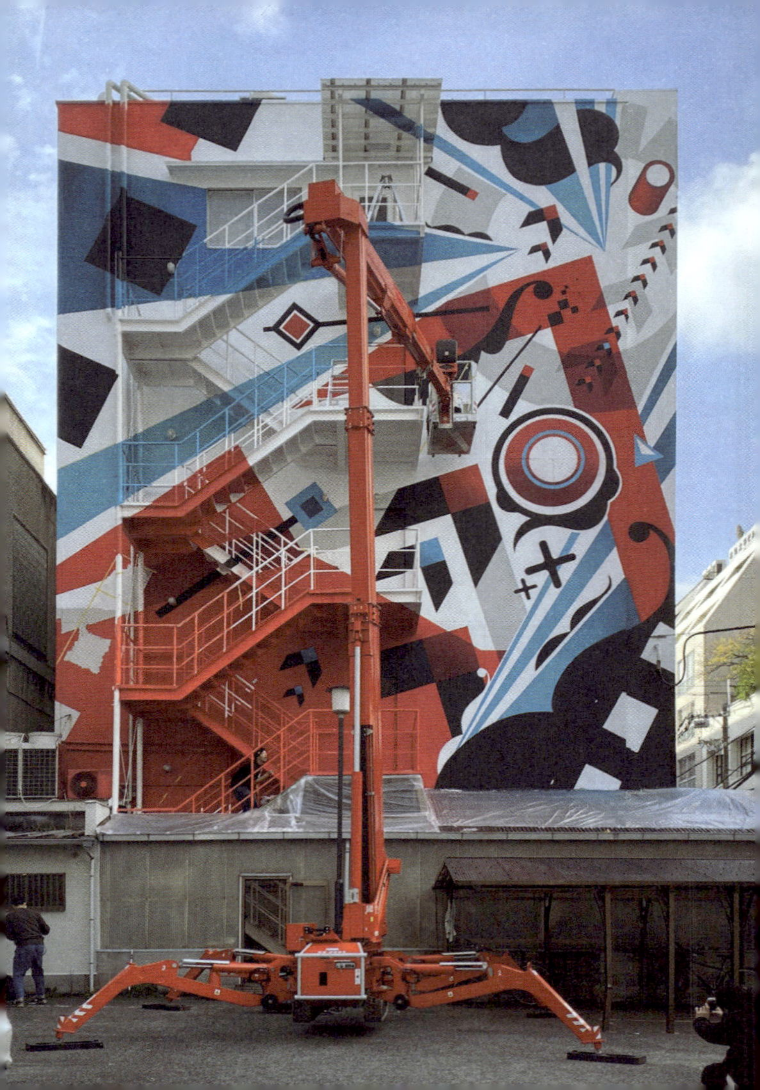

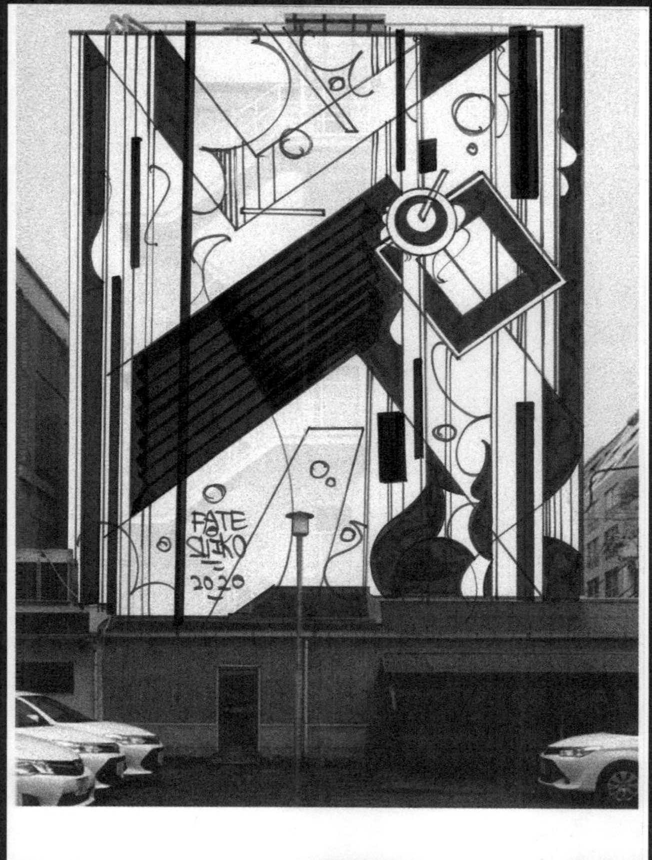

"BORN TO DARE" / SUIKO & FATE, Osaka, 2020

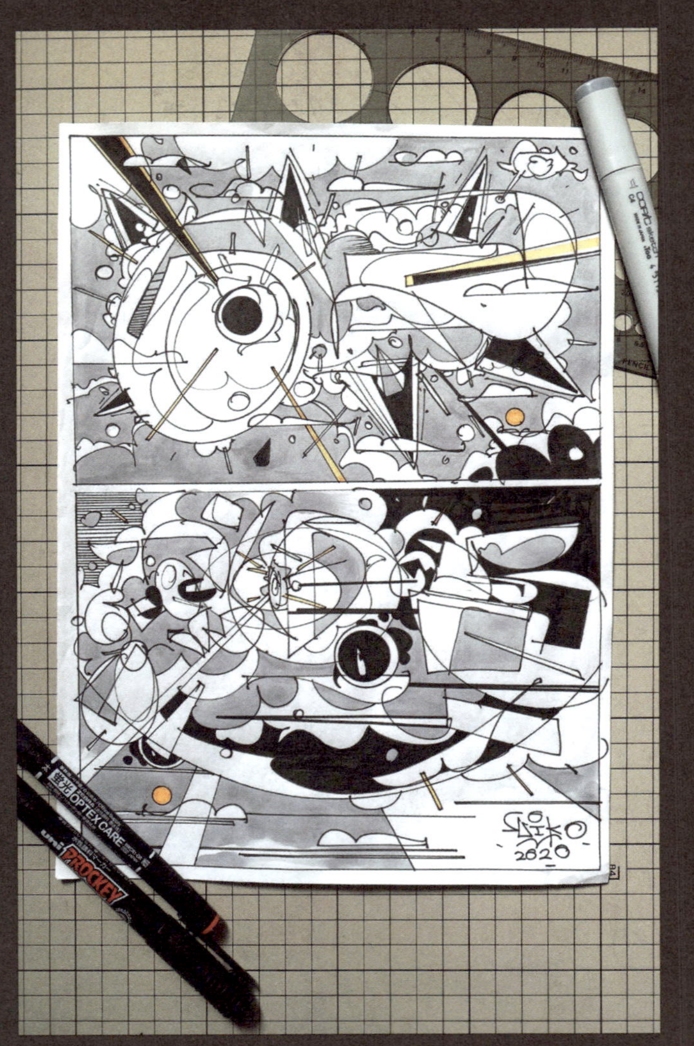

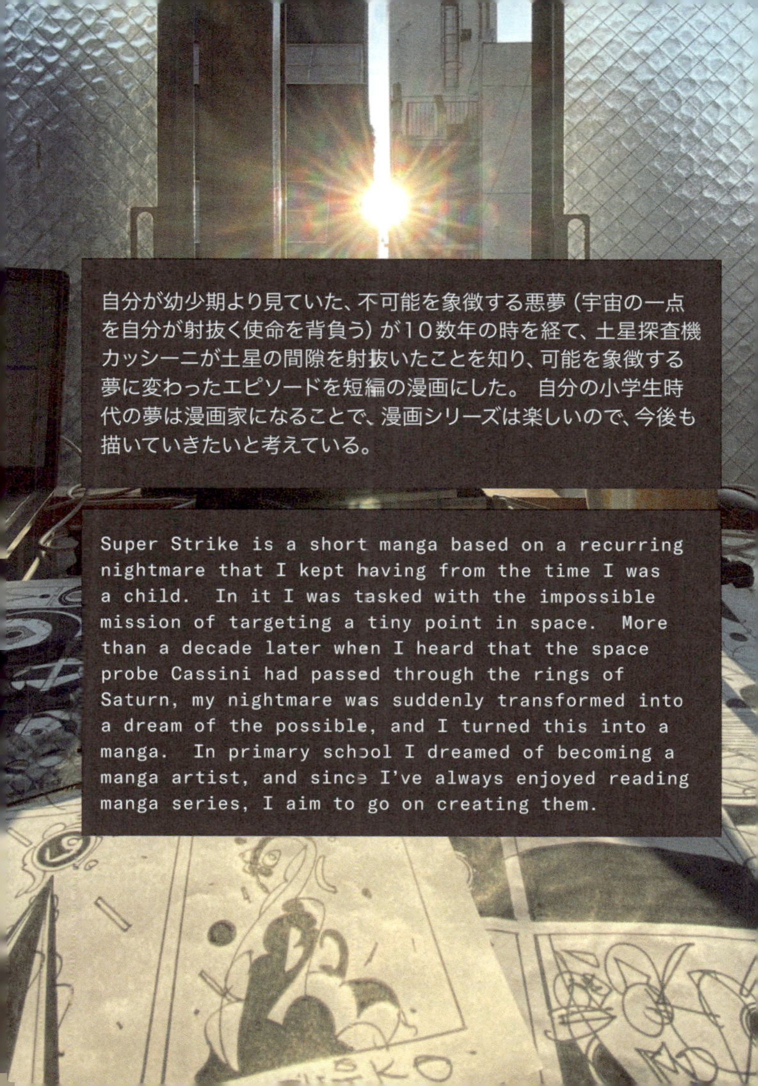

自分が幼少期より見ていた、不可能を象徴する悪夢（宇宙の一点を自分が射抜く使命を背負う）が１０数年の時を経て、土星探査機カッシーニが土星の間隙を射抜いたことを知り、可能を象徴する夢に変わったエピソードを短編の漫画にした。 自分の小学生時代の夢は漫画家になることで、漫画シリーズは楽しいので、今後も描いていきたいと考えている。

Super Strike is a short manga based on a recurring nightmare that I kept having from the time I was a child. In it I was tasked with the impossible mission of targeting a tiny point in space. More than a decade later when I heard that the space probe Cassini had passed through the rings of Saturn, my nightmare was suddenly transformed into a dream of the possible, and I turned this into a manga. In primary school I dreamed of becoming a manga artist, and since I've always enjoyed reading manga series, I aim to go on creating them.

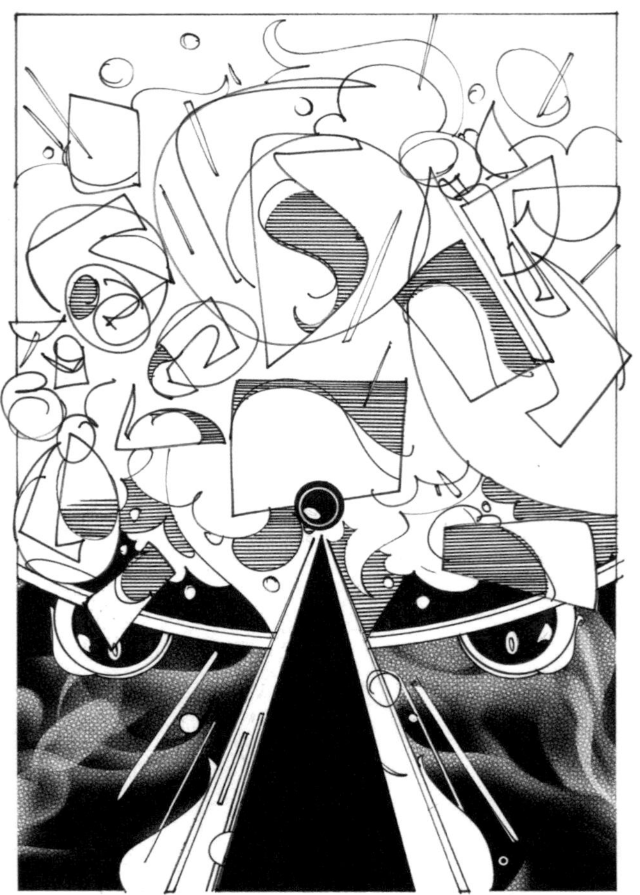

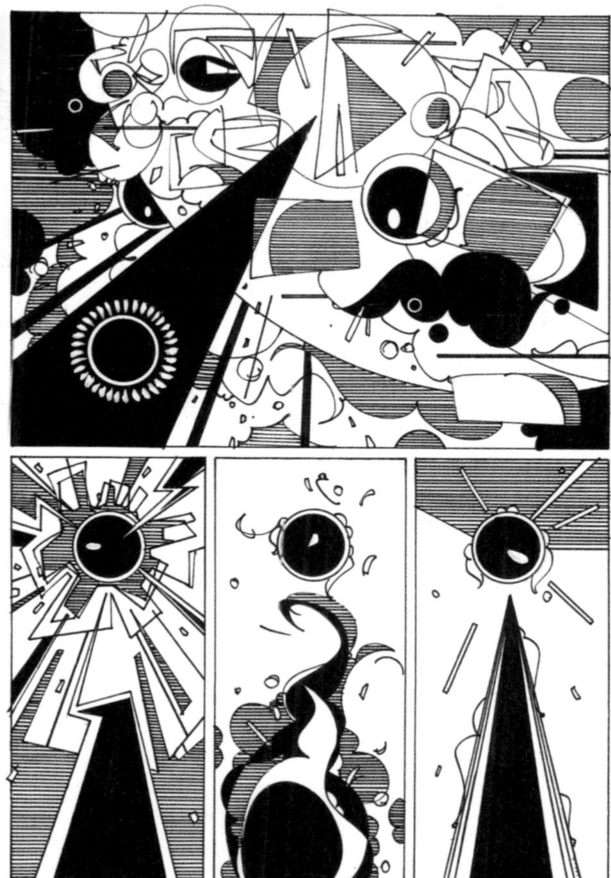

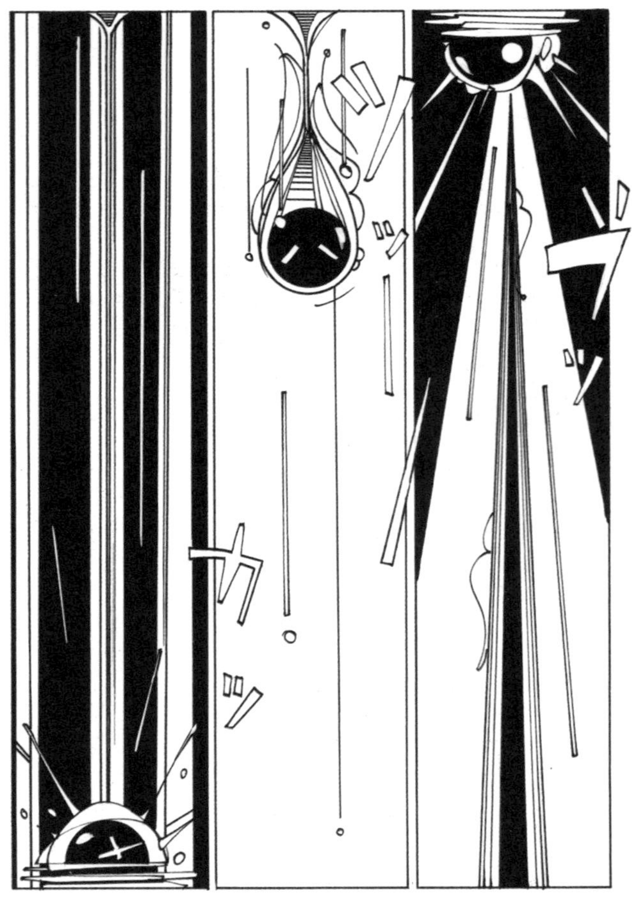

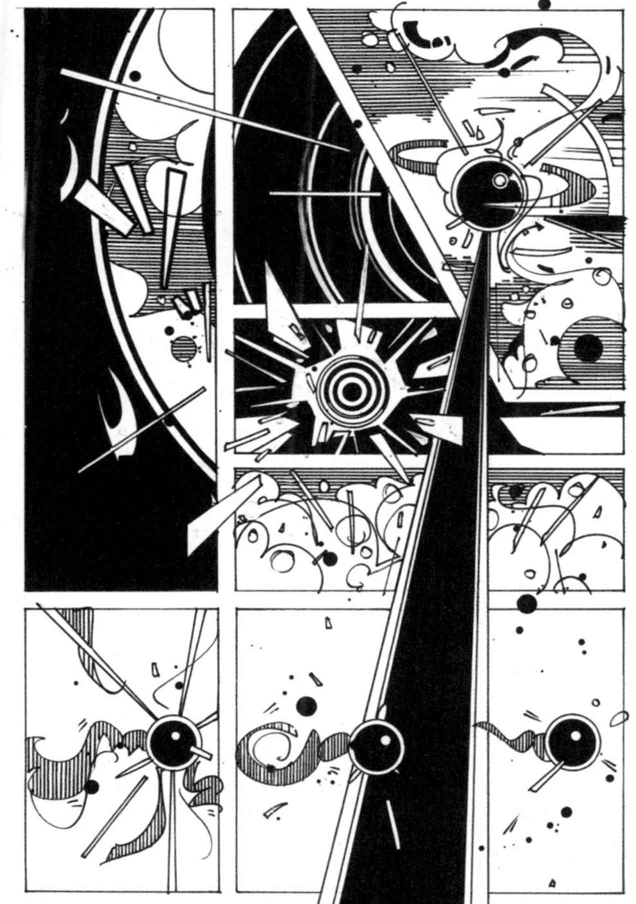

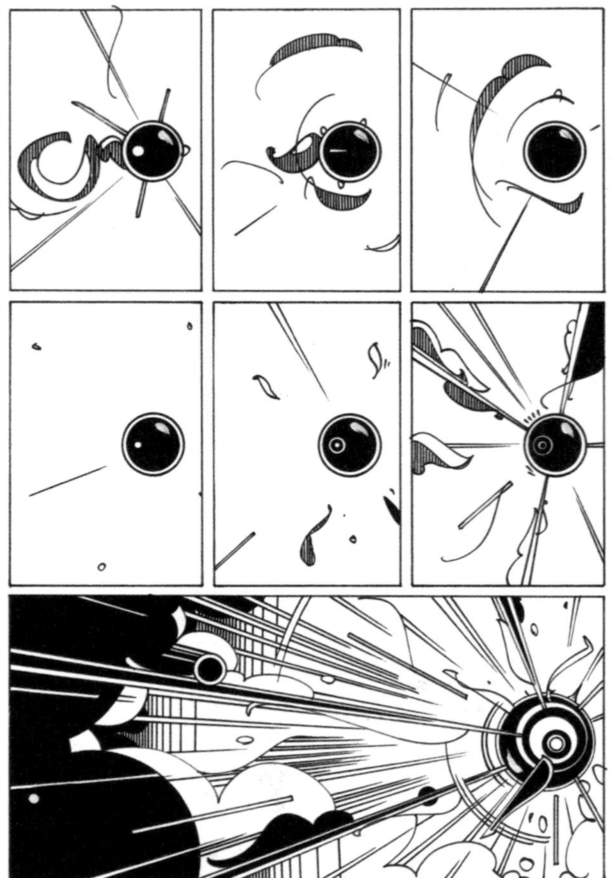

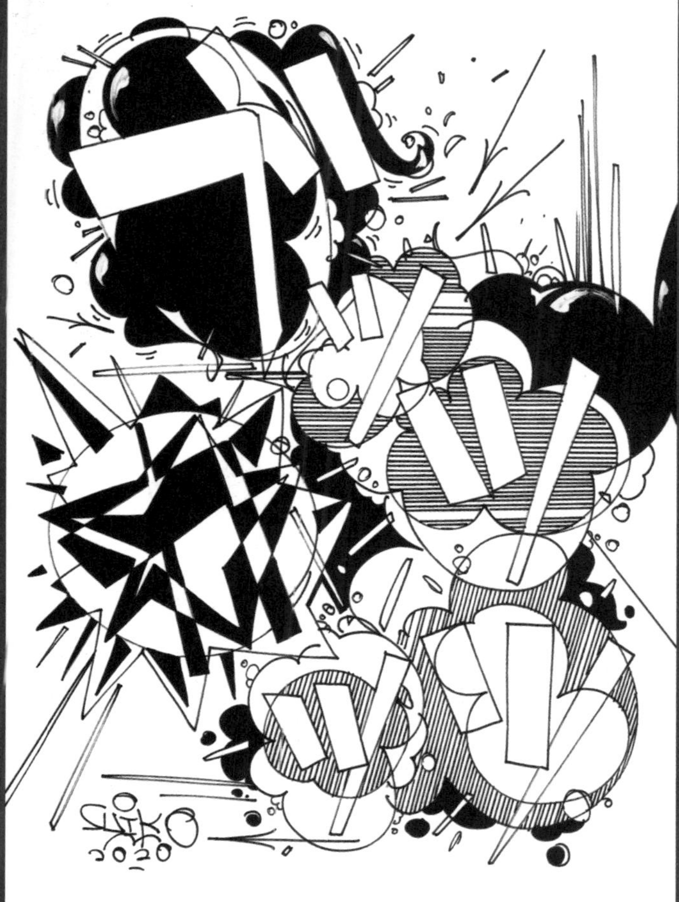

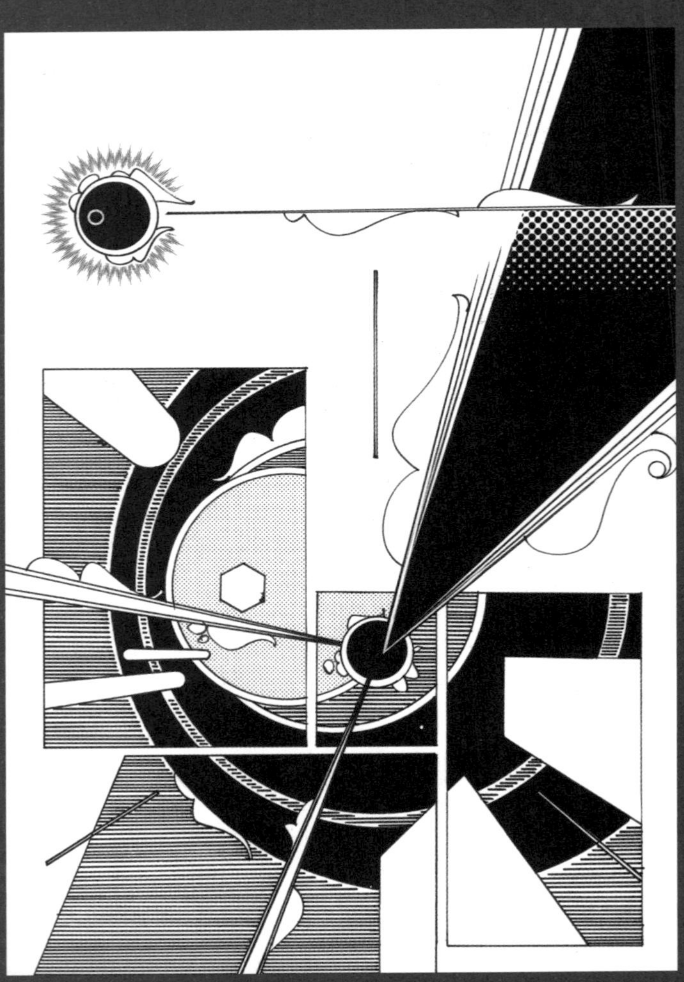

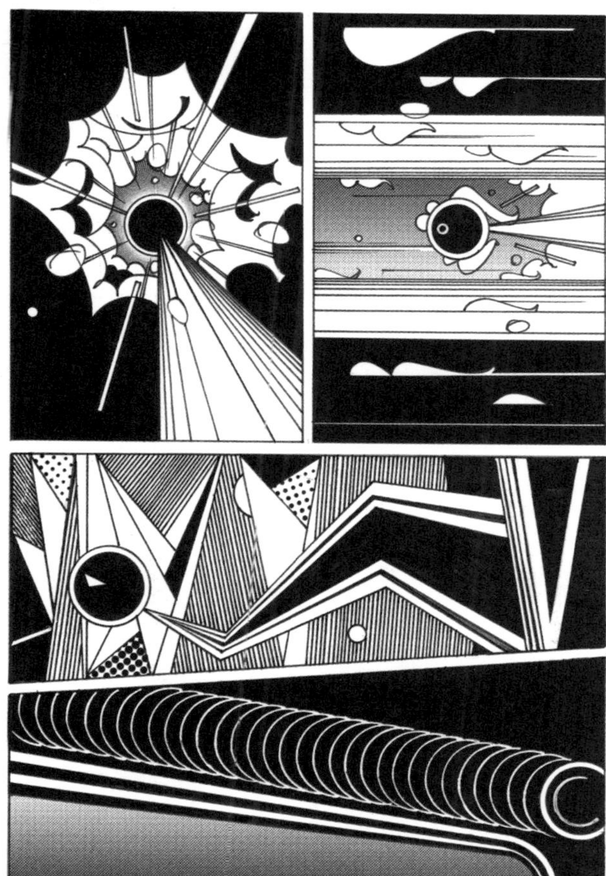

CB-348 WAX TYPE ADHESIVE

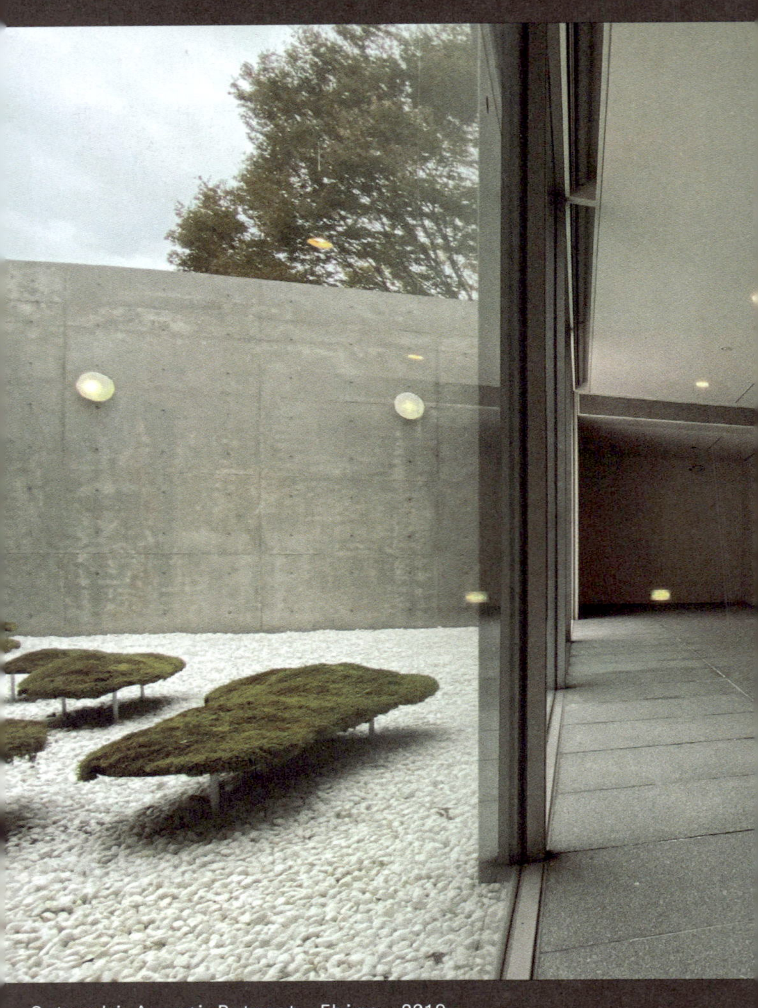

Setouchi Aonagi Retreat, Ehime, 2019

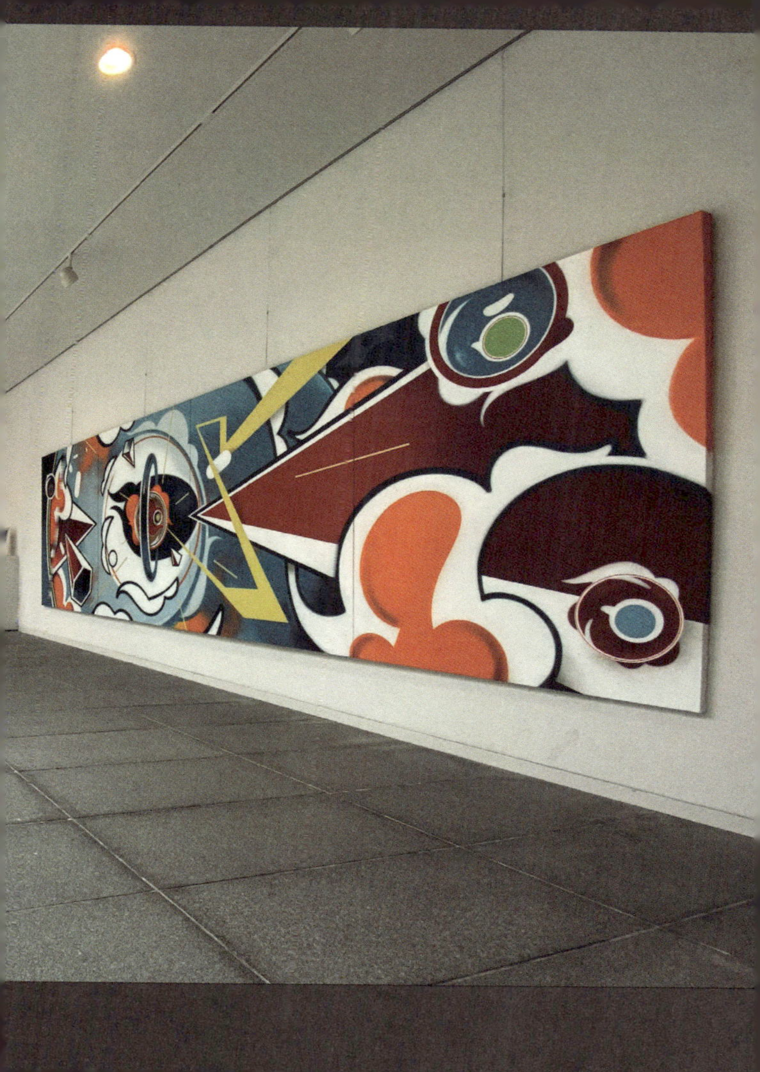

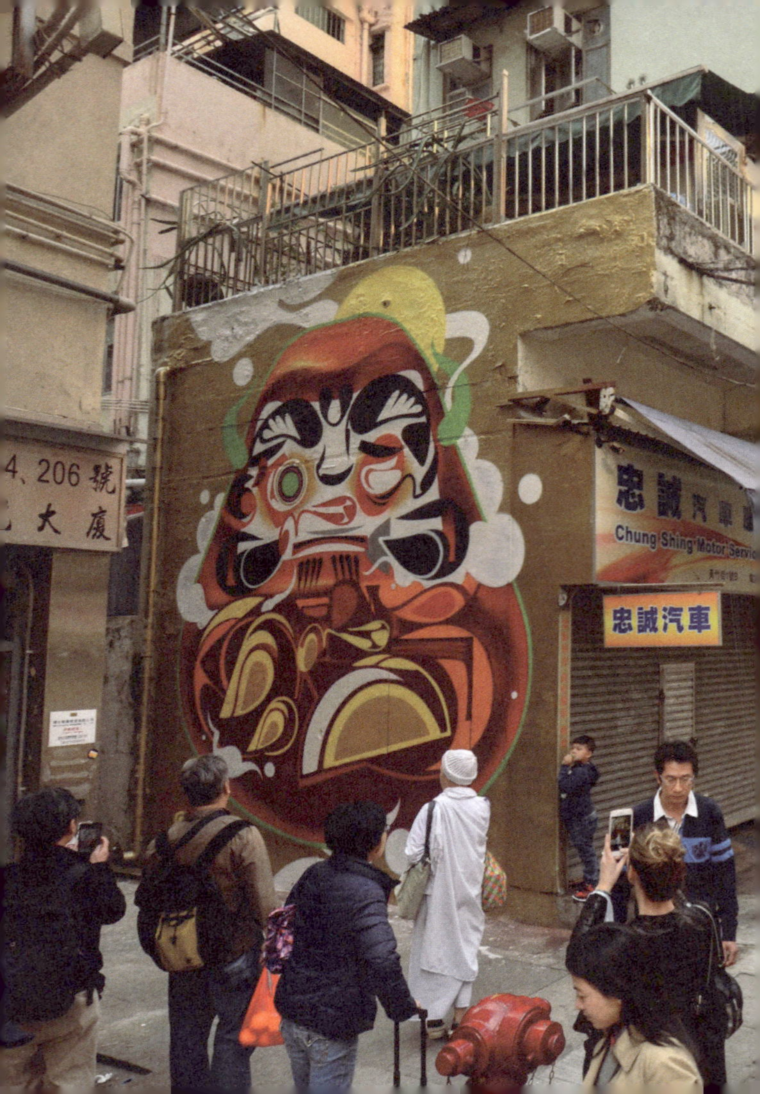
4, 206 號
大廈
忠誠汽車
Chung Shing Motor Servic
忠誠汽車

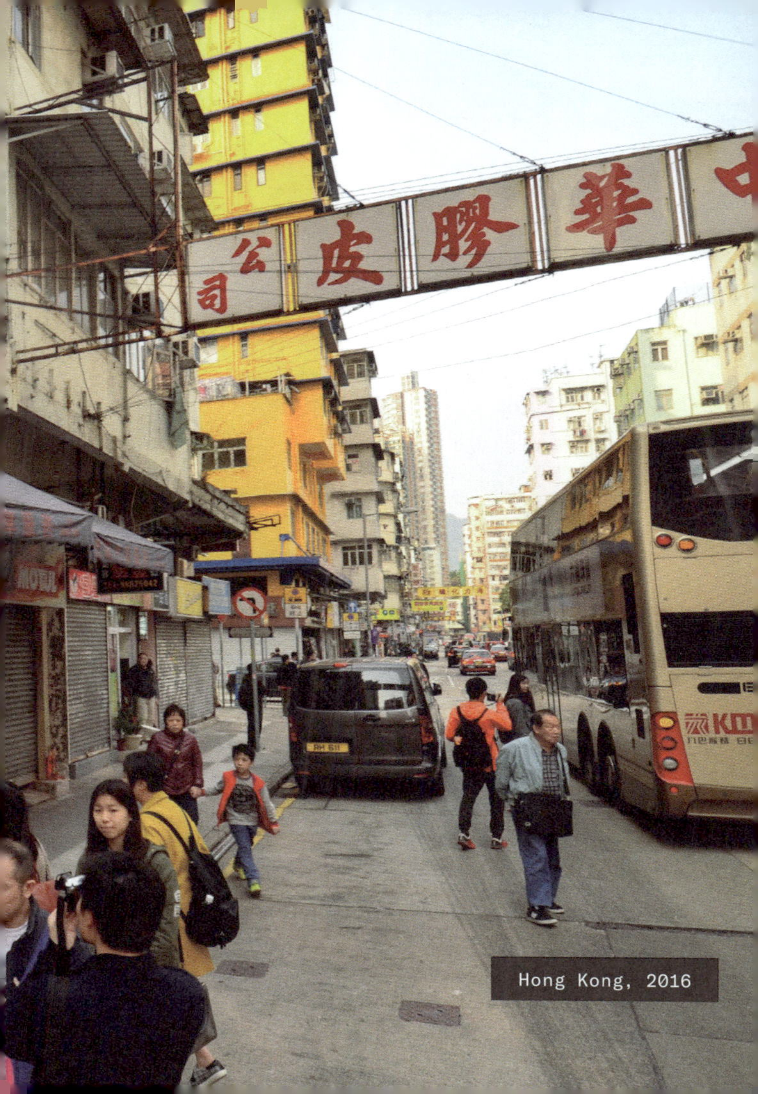

Hong Kong, 2016

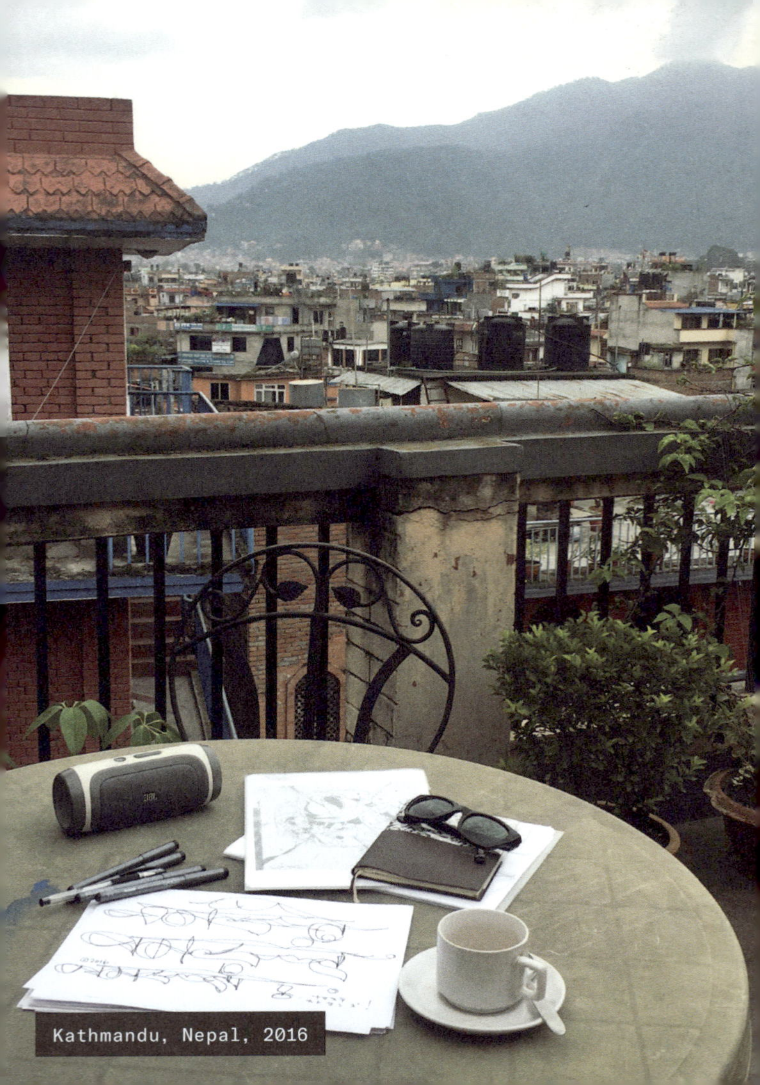
Kathmandu, Nepal, 2016

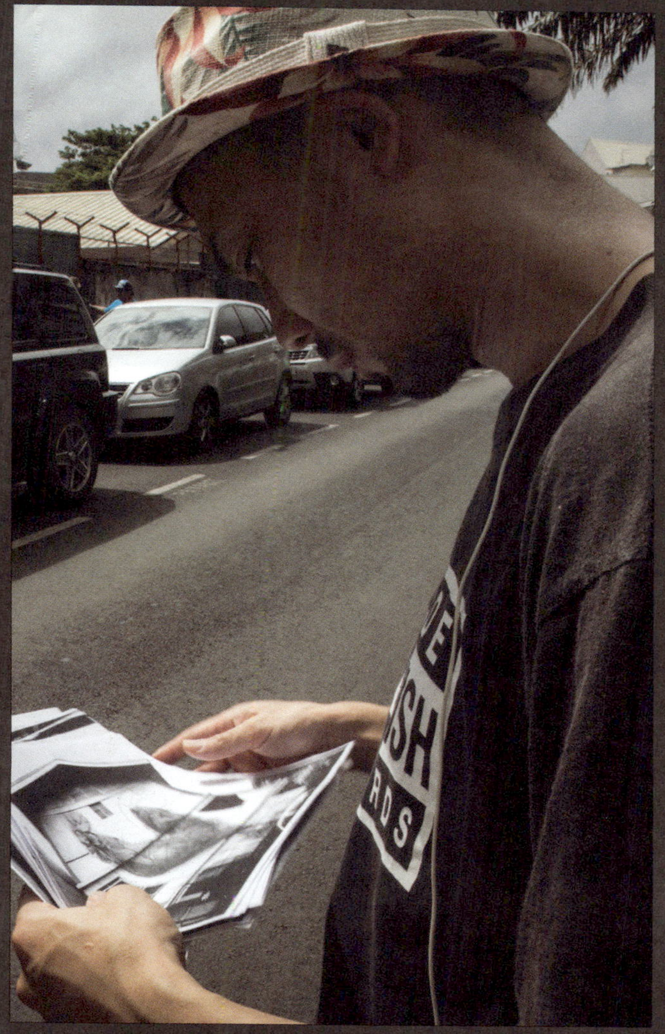
SH
RDS

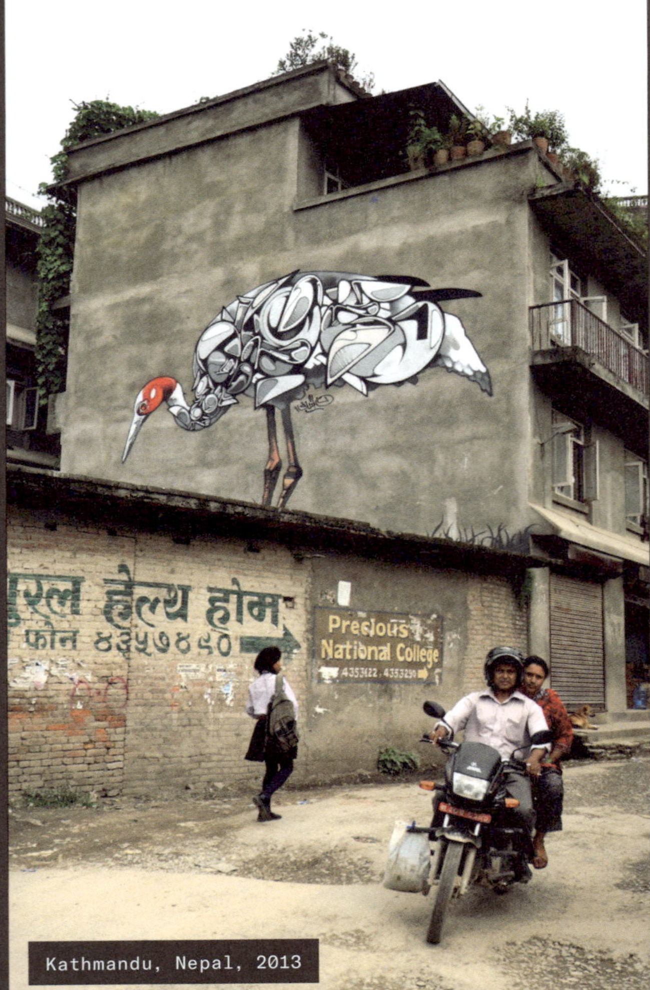

Kathmandu, Nepal, 2013

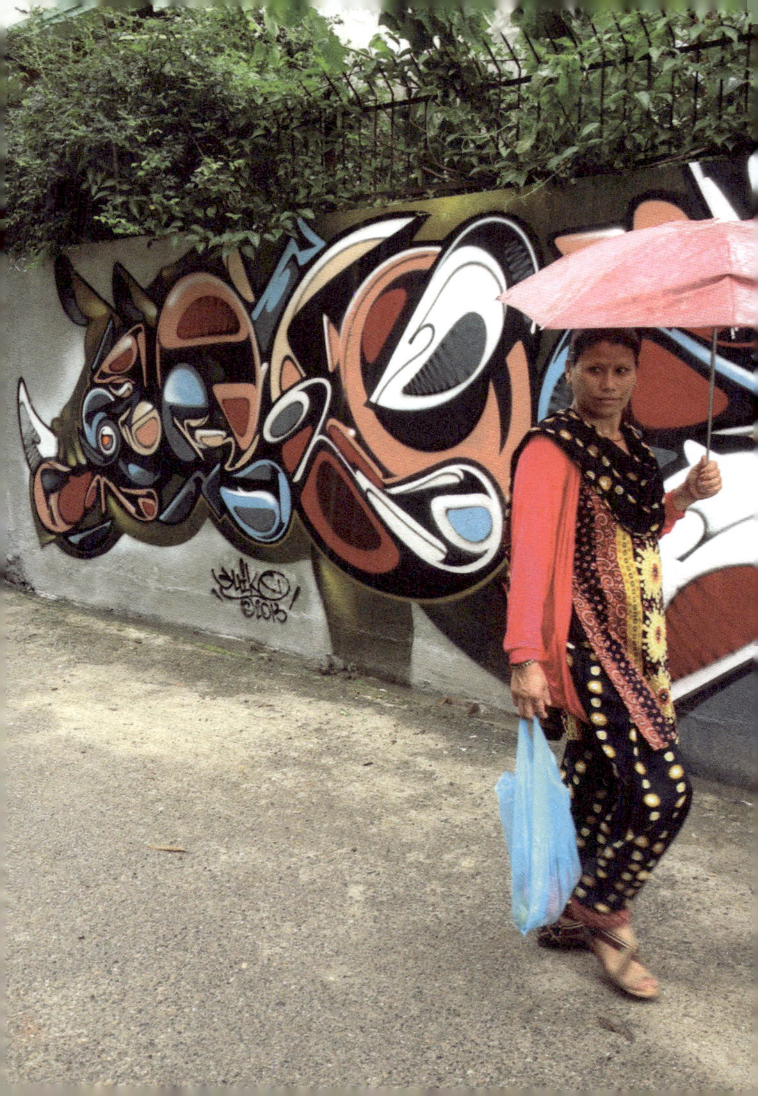

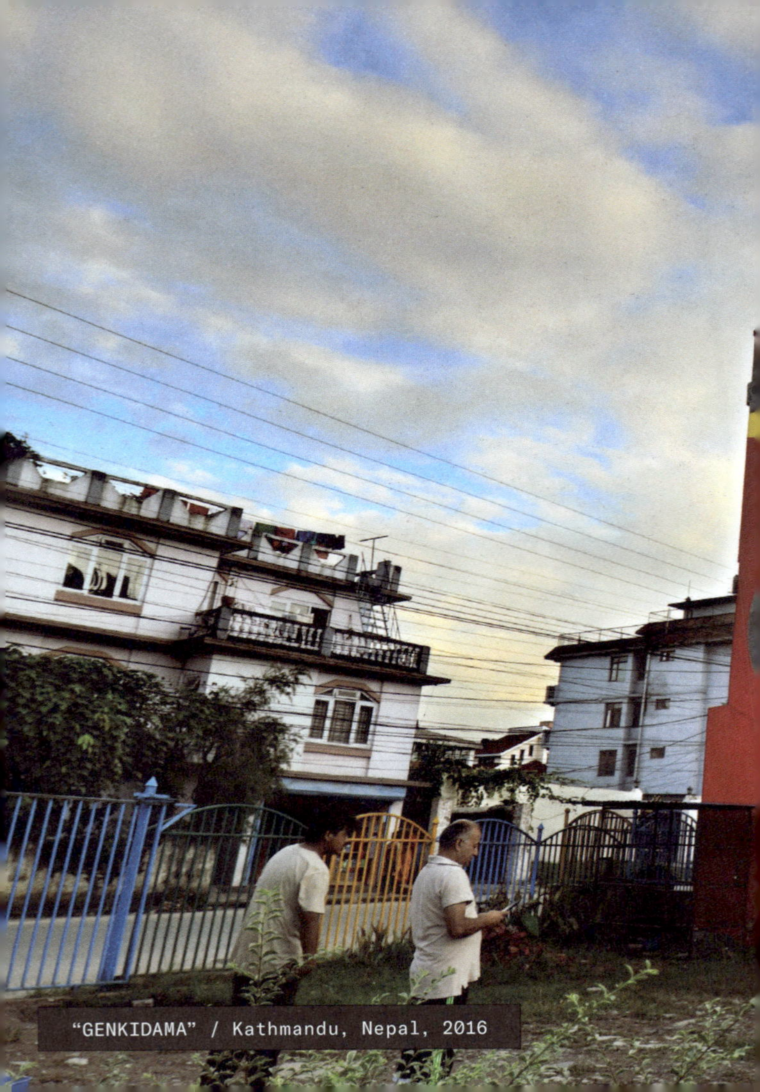

"GENKIDAMA" / Kathmandu, Nepal, 2016

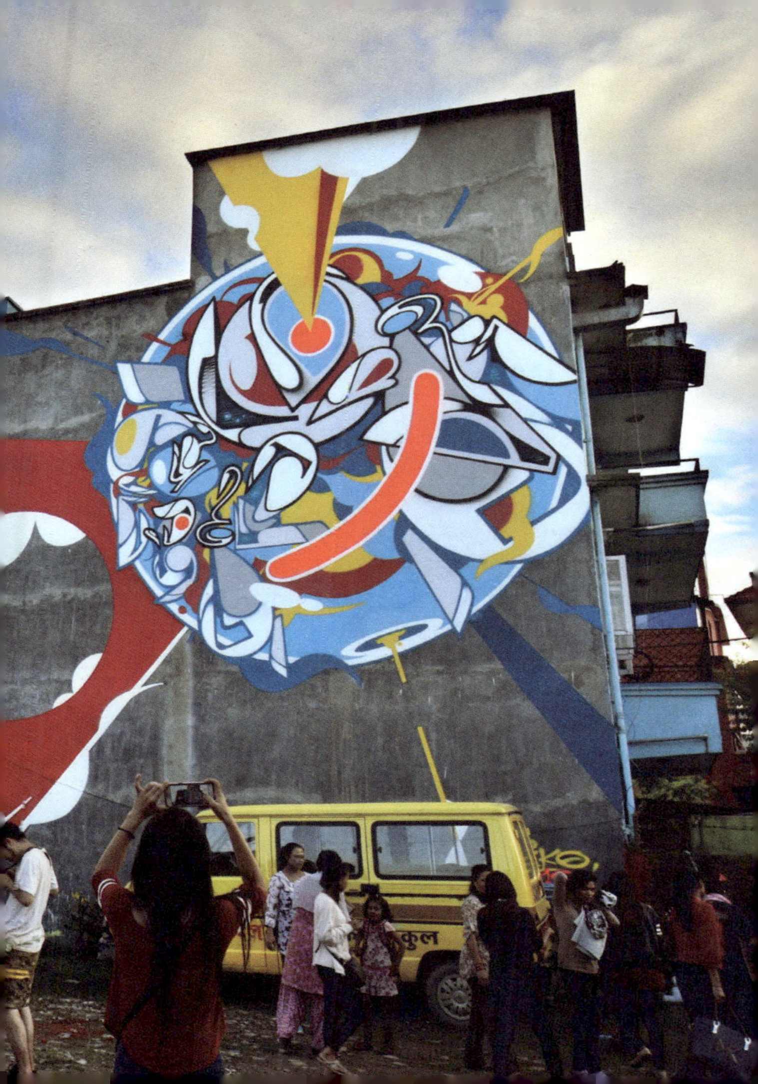

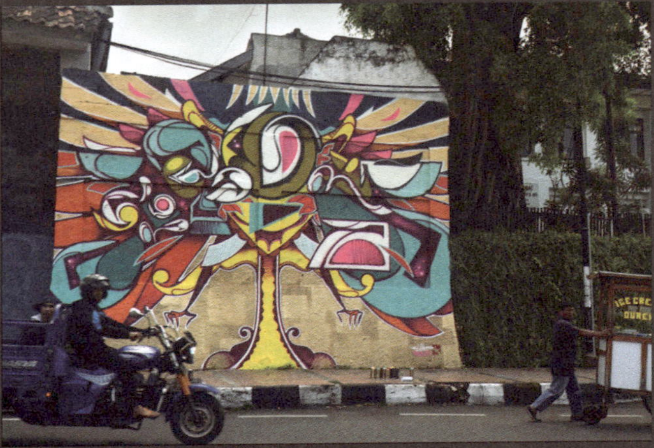

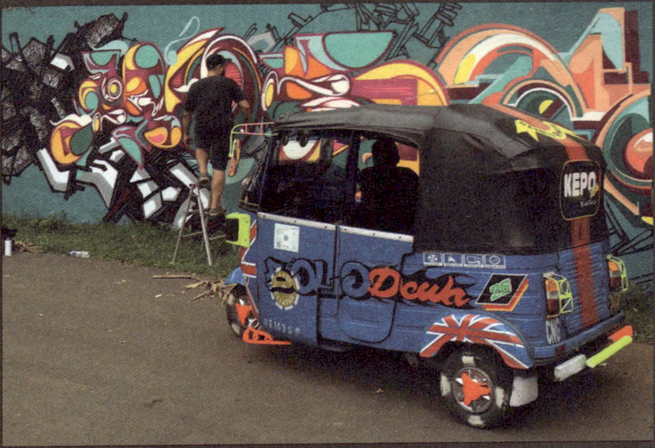

SUIKO, DARBOTZ, TUTU / Jakarta, Indonesia, 2016

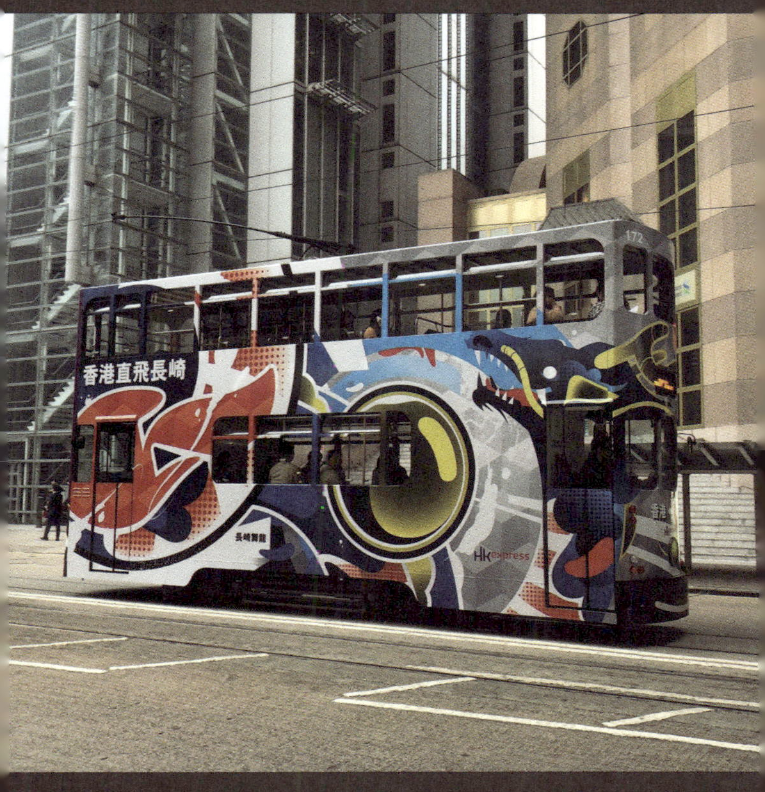

Hong Kong, 2019

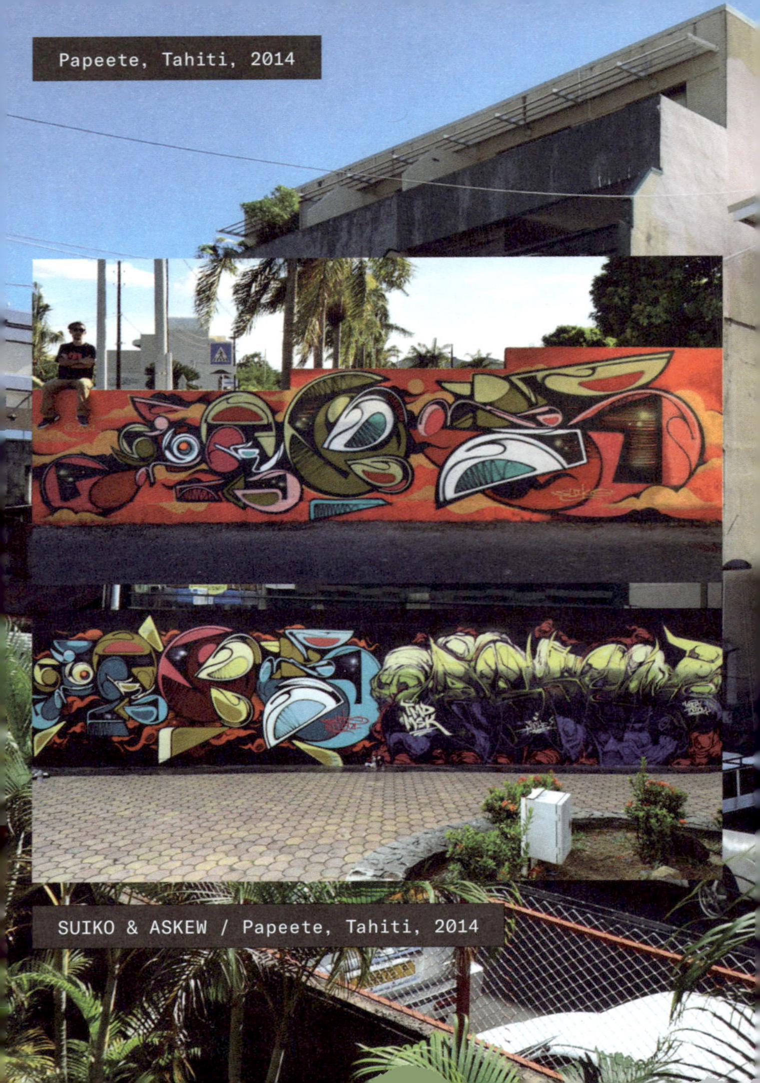

SUIKO & ASKEW / Papeete, Tahiti, 2014

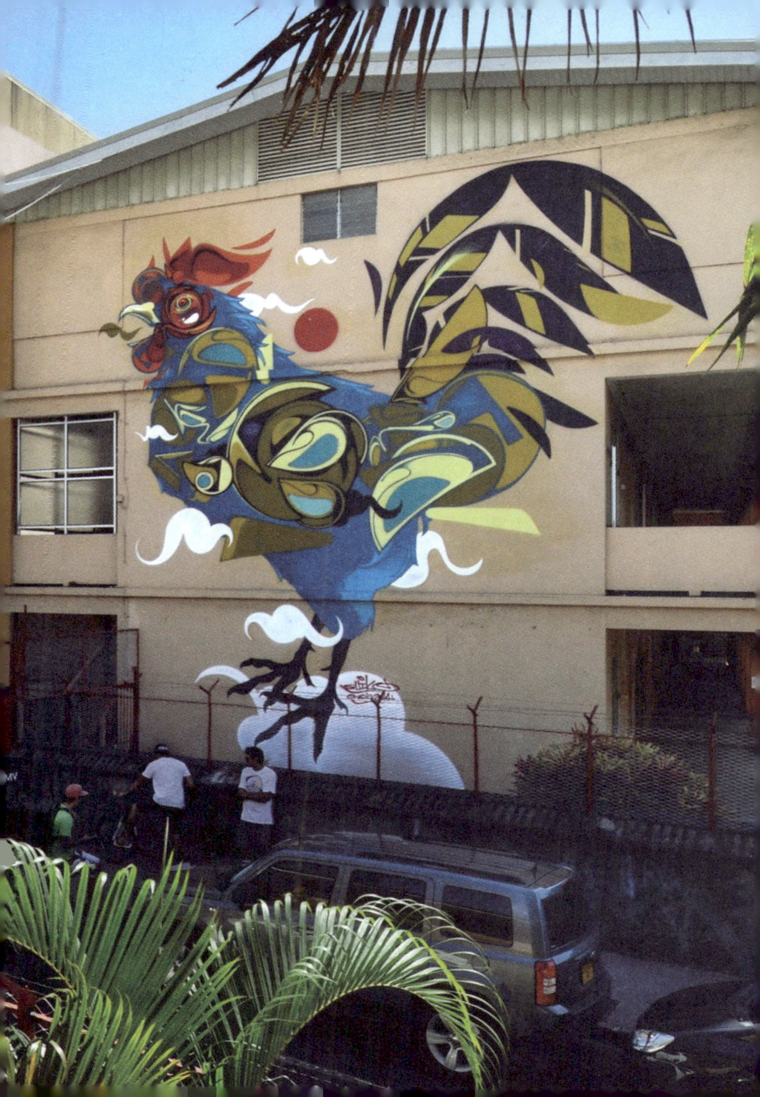

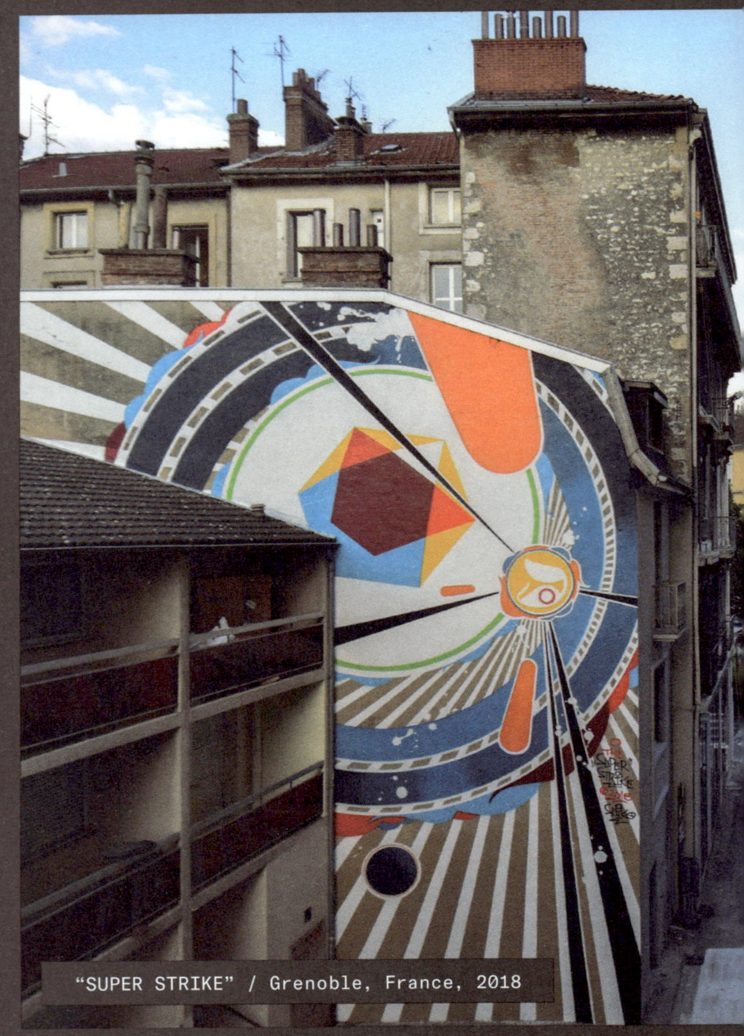

"SUPER STRIKE" / Grenoble, France, 2018

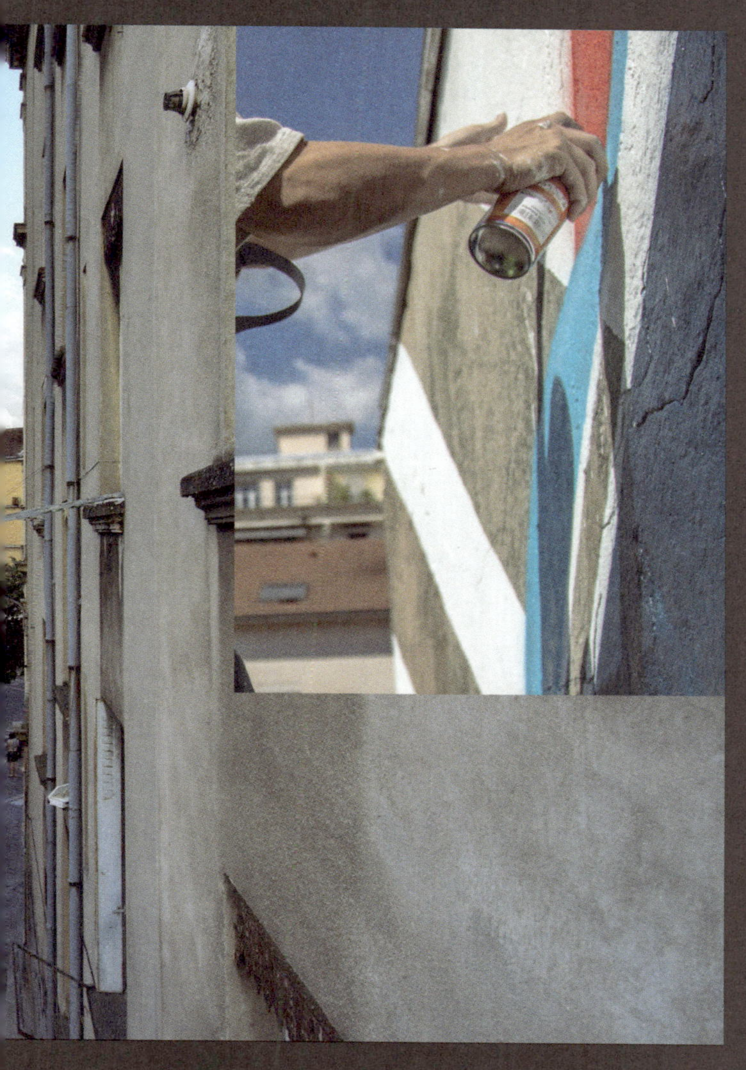

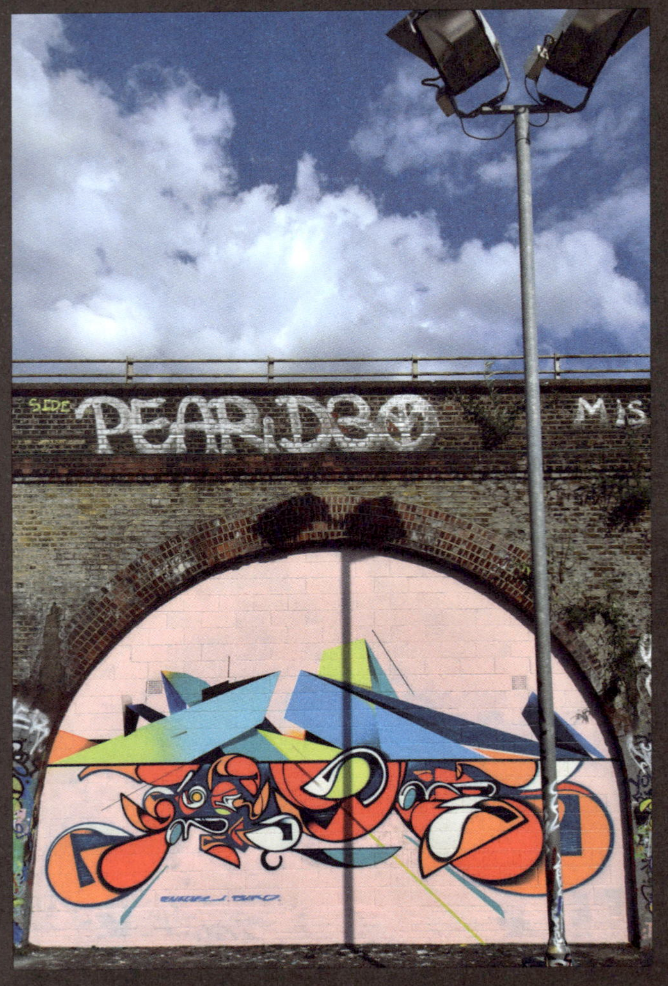

SUIKO & REMI ROUGH, London, U.K., 2017

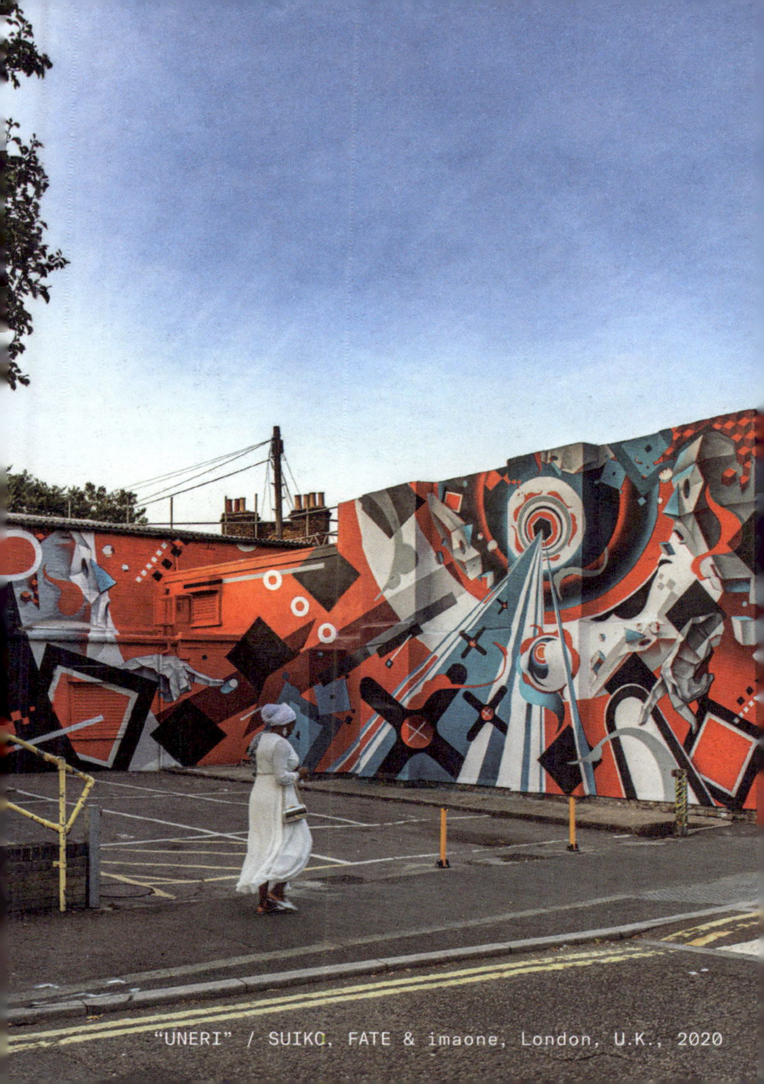

"UNERI" / SUIKO, FATE & imaone, London, U.K., 2020

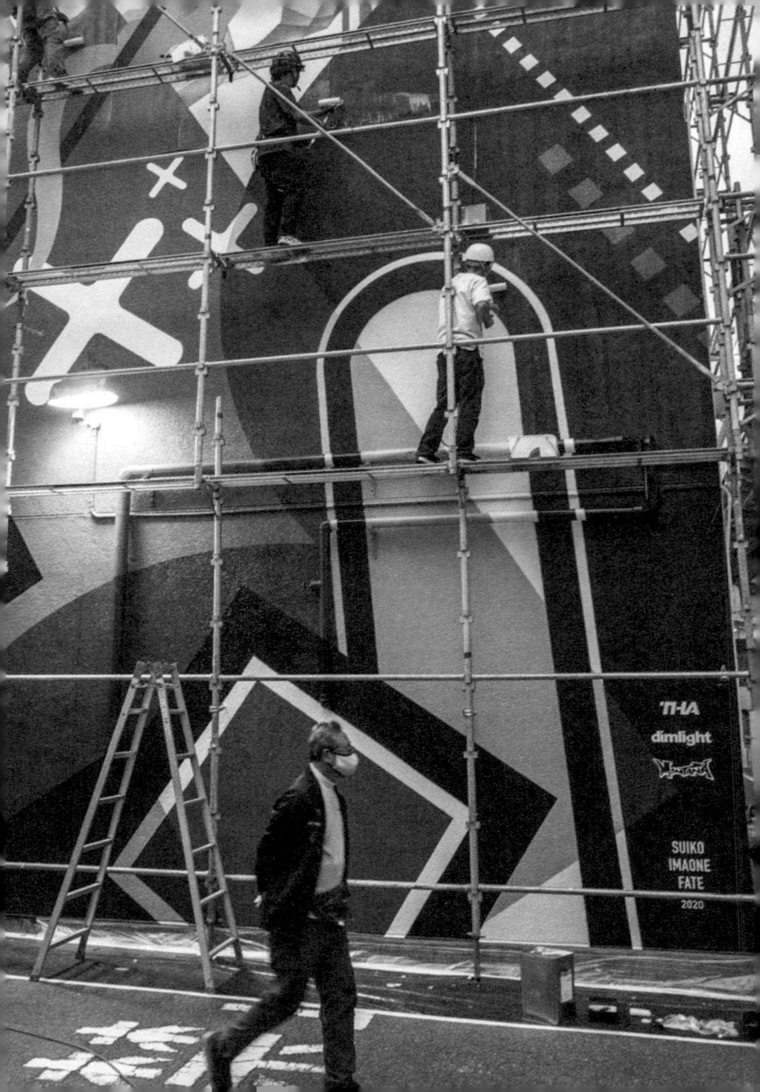

THA
dimlight
SUIKO
IMAONE
FATE
2020

Photography by:

SUIKO / @suiko1
Louie Marino / @cool_h4nd_lou
Wallshare / @wallshare
SUKIMA / @sukima.jp
SHUTIE / @shutieone
Yuichi Ueno / @ueno4to
kleptomaniac / @kptm1979
Selina Miles / @selinamiles
HKexpress / @hk_express
Andrea Berlese / @andreaberlesephotography
Yuta Fukuda / @yutafukuda.uk